THE WORKS OF ST. PATRICK

ST. SECUNDINUS
HYMN ON ST. PATRICK

TRANSLATED AND ANNOTATED

BY

LUDWIG BIELER, PH. D.

Lecturer in Palaeography and Classics
University College, Dublin

WESTMINSTER, MARYLAND

THE NEWMAN PRESS

LONDON

LONGMANS, GREEN AND CO.

1953

THE NEWMAN PRESS
WESTMINISTER MD USA

LONGMANS, GREEN AND CO LTD
6 & 7 CLIFFORD STREET LONDON W I
BOSTON HOUSE STRAND STREET CAPE TOWN
531 LITTLE COLLINS STREET MELBOURNE

ORIENT LONGMANS LTD
BOMBAY CALCUTTA MADRAS

First published in the U. S. A. 1953
First published in Great Britain 1953

De licentia Superioris Ordinis. Nihil obstat: J. QUASTEN, cens. dep.
Imprimatur: PATRICIUS A. O'BOYLE, D.D., Archiep. Washingtonen., d. 19 Maii 1952

PRINTED IN THE UNITED STATES OF AMERICA
BY YORK COMPOSITION CO., INC., YORK, PA.

CONTENTS

THE WORKS OF ST. PATRICK

INTRODUCTION

THE LIFE AND WRITINGS OF ST. PATRICK

1

St. Patrick—Magonus Sucatus Patricius, to give him his full name—was born about 385 in some unknown town of Roman Britain.[1] He was the son of a certain Calpornius[2] and his wife Concessa.[3] Patrick's father appears to have been a member of the city council (*decurio*)[4] and thus a man of some social standing. He was probably advanced in years when he took holy orders as his father (Patrick's grandfather) Potitus had done before him. Potitus had been a priest, Calpornius was a deacon. Both had probably joined the clergy for the same motive, common in those days: to escape the increasing financial burden of municipal office.[5] The atmosphere in Patrick's home and social surroundings was, as he himself attests, anything but religious.[6]

Calpornius seems to have been a newcomer to the city where he resided. His native place is given in the manuscripts of Patrick's *Confession* as Bannauem Taburniae (of uncertain location, probably near the sea, in the southwest); he still owned the family estate which was situated in its vicinity. Here Patrick was captured by Irish raiders at the age of sixteen and sold as a slave in Ireland.[7] Irish tradition of the seventh century (Muirchú, Tírechán) has it that Patrick served the druid Miliuc maccu Boin near Slemish, Co. Antrim.

Up to the time of his captivity, Patrick had led the life

3

of a somewhat irresponsible lad of the upper classes. He
went worldly ways and turned a deaf ear to the admoni-
tions of the clergy. At school he seems to have cared
more for games than grammar. On one occasion he
sinned gravely, and this seriously troubled his conscience
in later years.[8]

In the solitude of Slemish, tending the flocks of a " barbarian " master, Patrick found God. He patiently endured
the hardships of his servitude and led a life of prayer and
voluntary mortification.[9] At the end of six years he heard
a voice in his dreams, announcing God's forgiveness and
bidding him to go to his country and his people; a ship,
the voice indicated, was waiting to take him home. He
had to walk two hundred miles before he found the ship
which the voice of his dream had promised him; it was a
boat carrying Irish hounds to the continent.[10]

A detail in Patrick's story of his escape may be of some
help in establishing its date. After their arrival in Gaul
the crew, with their hounds, travelled twenty-eight days
through " desert." This would point to a date after sum-
mer, 407, when Gaul was occupied by the usurper Constantine III; conceivably the Irish traders may have
by-passed inhabited localities for fear of encounters with
Constantine's soldiery.[11]

When and how Patrick managed to return to Britain
we do not know. He seems to have found his parents still
at his old home.[12] They naturally urged him to stay with
them; but Patrick became more and more convinced that
he was called by God to convert his former masters. In a
dream he heard the voice of the Irish calling him back, and
his dream was confirmed by spiritual experiences which

Patrick describes in words deliberately borrowed from St. Paul.[13]

For his religious training Patrick went to Gaul.[14] He became attached to the church of Auxerre, under its famous bishop Germanus. Here he took seriously to learning — a hard thing for a man no longer in the prime of his youth, who had to make up for his ill-spent and drastically interrupted school days. Besides, Patrick was born a man of action with little inclination for study. His scholarly achievements, to judge from his writings, were modest enough; all the more intense, it seems, was his spiritual life; and in due course he rose to the diaconate.[15]

During these years Patrick never lost sight of his ultimate goal — the conversion of the Irish. His opportunity came when in 429 Palladius, a native of Gaul and at the time archdeacon of Pope Celestine, recommended sending Germanus as papal legate to Britain for the purpose of combating a revival of Pelagianism.[16] In carrying out his mission, Germanus had to consider also the affairs of Ireland, whose small and scattered Christian communities naturally looked to the clergy of Britain for guidance. In the circumstances it seemed best to give the Irish a bishop of their own. Patrick's name was mentioned in the question of choice. One friend at least openly declared that he should be elected. Patrick's superiors, however, had their doubts. This well-disposed, but half-educated Briton was scarcely the sort of man to be recommended for such a responsible office.[17] Germanus went to Britain, and among the men accompanying him was Patrick's friend. At some British synod the question of the Irish episcopate was raised, and Patrick was mentioned as a candidate. But opposition was strong, and finally even Patrick's friend

went over to it. He went so far as to disclose Patrick's
early sin which the latter had confided to him in a moment
of spiritual anguish before he was ordained deacon. The
synod rejected Patrick and nominated Palladius.[18]

In 431 Palladius was sent with papal authority to the
Irish as their first bishop.[19] On his way to the channel
ports he had to pass through Auxerre. He may have taken
the opportunity of conferring with Germanus about Patrick's future. At any rate, we find Patrick, accompanied
by a senior, the presbyter Segitius, on his way to Ireland
in the following year. At Eburobrica (the modern
Avrolles), however, they received the news that Palladius
was dead; they returned to Auxerre, and Patrick was now
consecrated bishop.[20] He made for his destination without
delay. The Irish Annals date Patrick's arrival as falling in
the year 432.[21]

Our knowledge of the missionary work of St. Patrick is
derived mainly from passages in his own writings and from
a circular letter which contains canons drawn up by him
together with the bishops Auxilius and Iserninus.[22] Something can be gleaned also from the hymn on St. Patrick
ascribed to St. Secundinus, who, with the two bishops just
mentioned, had joined Patrick as an auxiliary bishop in
439.[23] In the seventh-century documents and the later
Lives of St. Patrick deriving from them, truth is almost in-
extricably mixed with legend.

Some facts at least stand out.[24] Patrick concentrated his
energies on the conversion of the princes, knowing that
their subjects would follow their example. With the
years, he relied more and more on a native clergy, re-
cruited mainly from the local nobility. In adapting the
organisation of the Roman Church to the conditions of

Ireland, where there were no cities, he seems to have made the *tuatha* (states) [25] his dioceses; the episcopal sees, called *civitates*, were probably organised on a quasi-monastic pattern. Being himself a lover of monasticism, he transmitted this love to the Irish.[26]

From the documents of the seventh century it would appear that Patrick began his mission in the north, where he was known from his early days; that he then turned to the west and south-west, and finally to the partly Christianised south-east. His metropolitan see he certainly erected in the north, at Armagh. The date of its foundation as given in the Annals of Ulster (444) is gravely suspect; it probably falls in the last years of his life.[27] That he exercised authority over the other bishops may be seen from his censure of the bishops of Mag Ái (Fragment 2).

Patrick's task was by no means easy. He met with strong opposition on the part of the druids and, it would seem, also of the older generation among the ruling class. He speaks of twelve dangers to his life [28] and declares that he has to face the possibility of martyrdom.[29] Even among his fellow Christians, in Ireland as well as in Britain and on the continent, he had severe critics. In his native Britain feeling against him was particularly strong; it flared up violently when, at some unknown date, he demanded the excommunication of the Welsh prince Coroticus, who during a reprisal raid against the Irish had massacred or captured a number of Patrick's neophytes.

Under the year 441 the Irish Annals record Patrick's " approval in the Catholic faith " by the new pope, Leo I. Nothing is known regarding the form and circumstances of this act. There certainly is no evidence to show that Patrick made a journey to Rome for the occasion.[30]

According to a seventh-century tradition, Patrick died at Saul in Ulster on March 17, 461. He had the satisfaction of leaving Ireland, which thirty years before had been largely pagan, as a country that had virtually become Christian.

2

St. Patrick was not a man of letters. Whatever he wrote was wrested from him by the circumstances of his life and the demands of his episcopal office. What remains of his writings are two complete letters, some fragments from other letters, and — probably his own in good part — a set of canons or rules of ecclesiastical discipline. These, together with the hymn of St. Secundinus in honour of St. Patrick and the so-called *Lorica* of St. Patrick, are the earliest documents of the Irish Church that have survived.

Among the works that have at one time or other been attributed to St. Patrick, the following have a claim to authenticity:

1. The *Confession*. The title, though not found in our earliest manuscripts, may be considered authentic. Note the use of the word in the last two paragraphs of the letter, and especially in the last: " This is my *confession* before I die." Patrick wrote his *Confession* in his old age (*in senectute mea*, 10), after many years of missionary work in Ireland (35 ff.), at a time when a man would naturally direct his thoughts to the end of his life.[31] The *Confession* was doubtless written in Ireland (1, 62).

In form, the *Confession* of St. Patrick is an open letter. It combines three main themes: thanksgiving to God for

His guidance and graces, a justification of Patrick's episcopate before his critics, and a frank confession of his sinful youth and his human weaknesses. These three ideas can all be expressed by the word *confessio;* they are eminently present in, for instance, the *Confessions* of St. Augustine, which Patrick seems to have known.[32] St. Patrick's apology is modelled on that of St. Paul to the Corinthians, with many deliberate verbal borrowings.[33] His addressees are not easy to determine. Criticism of St. Patrick's mission was voiced, it seems, not only in Ireland, but also in his native Britain, and even in Gaul. Patrick does not indicate against which opponents in particular this or that passage is directed. The "gentlemen scholars" (*dominicati rhetorici*) of *Confession* 13 are almost certainly to be sought in Gaul; those "learned in Law and Sacred Scripture" with whose unhampered progress in knowledge Patrick contrasts the vicissitudes of his own life (*Conf.* 9) are probably his countrymen; those who opposed his mission on the grounds of his rusticity (46) may be either the one or the other, and possibly both; the allegation of simony (37, 49 f., 61) might very well have originated in Ireland, perhaps as an attempt on the part of the druids to defame Patrick in the eyes of his flock; it is the same quarters from which objections would be voiced to his status as an alien (37).

From the factual point of view, the *Confession* of St. Patrick contains a good deal of autobiographical matter. It is indeed our main source, and certainly the sole authentic one, for the greater part of the saint's life. St. Patrick's main purpose in writing it was, however, neither autobiographical nor apologetic; we have it on his own authority (14) that he wanted to leave it to his Church as a spiritual bequest (*exagellias*).[34] The *Confession* is, first of all, a spiritual document; it centres round the " doxological " theme, to which all others are subsidiary. In fact, we get nowhere a coherent narration except in §§ 16–23; and even there Patrick dwells on a number of isolated events of spiritual significance and leaves all purely " external " factors in the dark. The important fact, for example, that the boat on which Patrick escaped from captivity had a cargo of racehounds — an essential detail for the understanding of § 18 — is stated only in passing on a later occasion (19). Apart from this short section, biographical details are introduced with no regard for chronology, as mere illustrations of the spiritual argument. For the historian this is particularly irritating in the paragraphs dealing with Patrick's rejection and rehabilitation (26–33), which are intelligible only in the light of the Auxerre traditions underlying Muirchú's *Life of St. Patrick*, 1.5–9.

Much the same is true of §§ 35–62, in which Patrick discusses his missionary work. We are given neither an historical sketch of his activities nor a systematic report. Many interesting points of missionary practice and ecclesiastical organisation are hardly touched; they are brought to light only by historical interpretation. The gaps in our knowledge are filled to some extent by the canons of Patricius, Auxilius, and Iserninus, the hymn on St. Patrick by St. Secundinus, and the traditions of the Patrician churches collected in the seventh century by Tírechán. Such an important subject as the liturgy of St. Patrick remains almost entirely unknown.[35] Of his theology we get at least a glimpse from his insistence on the Catholic doctrine of grace;[36] we are reminded of the fact that the Irish episcopate was established in connection with St. Germanus' mission against the Neo-Pelagians in Britain. The character of St. Patrick's Bible text is sufficiently manifested in his numerous Biblical quotations and allusions; it is Old Latin in the Old Testament, Vulgate (or nearly so) in Acts, and "mixed" in the other books of the New Testament.[37]

2. The *Letter to the Soldiers of Coroticus* ("*Epistle* ").
The title rests on no manuscript authority but is suggested by a passage in §2. Coroticus, a British prince, commonly identified with Ceredig, the founder of the Welsh principality of Cardigan, was obviously one of those local rulers on imperial territory who, after the breakdown of Roman rule, defended as best they could the remnants of Roman civilisation against the "barbarians." In Britain this situation existed since the withdrawal of Roman troops in 407. Even for some time past, south-western Britain had been a favourite target of Irish raiders; it is in one of these raids that young Patrick was taken captive. With the accession of Coroticus, things began to take a different turn; he not only defended the coast of Britain against raids from the neighbouring island, but occasionally ventured even on a reprisal raid. Nominal Christian though he was (§§2, 5, 6, 7, 14, 19, 21), it mattered very little to him whether the victims of his aggression were pagans or Christians. On one occasion a band of his soldiers had slaughtered a number of Patrick's neophytes at the baptismal altar and then abducted the rest of the congregation into slavery. A letter of remonstration, handed to the raiders by a delegation of clerics, had been received with open scorn (3). Patrick now demands the

excommunication of the guilty, and that of Coroticus himself, unless they do penance and restore the surviving victims to freedom; he also finds moving words for the
martyrs (17 f.) and the unfortunate prisoners, especially
the women, for whose innocence he has grave fears (15 f.,
19, 21).

The event, which is known only from St. Patrick's
letter, cannot be exactly dated. The rule of Coroticus
can be calculated only approximately by counting back,
in terms of generations, from the obits of later descendants.
A date in the forties of the fifth century is quite arguable.[38]
The letter which we read must have been written some
time after the event, when a number of the prisoners had
already been sold into slavery to the Picts (15); though
the emotional tone in Patrick's account of the incident (3)
and in his address of the dead victims (17 f.) shows that
the wound in his heart was still fresh. Relative to the
Confession, the *Letter* is almost certainly earlier. The
demanded excommunication of Coroticus, upon whom
the Roman Christians of Britain looked as their protector,
seems to have aroused anew the hostility to Patrick that
had resulted in his rejection. The *Confession* might very
well also be a reply to such opposition. The many verbal
parallels in the two works and their identical pattern of
composition may also be explained, at least in part, by the
fact that Patrick, before dictating his *Confession,* reread
his earlier manifesto.[39]

Again, as in the *Confession,* there is a constant change
of addressees: the soldiers of Coroticus (2, etc.), the
clergy of Britain (esp. 10 f.), the British Christians as a
whole (7, 13, 21), Coroticus in person (14), and, by a

naïve rhetorical fiction, even the victims themselves (17 f.).

3. Some other letters of Patrick are known only indirectly either from references or from scanty fragments. An earlier letter to the soldiers of Coroticus is mentioned in the one that has survived (*Epist.* 3). There are two fragments of unidentified letters, the second of which, concerning the bishops of Mag Ái, is of considerable interest as the sole remaining evidence of Patrick's exercise of metropolitan jurisdiction.

4. The *Book of Armagh*, a manuscript written *c.* 807, contains three, or possibly four, "*Sayings of Patrick.*" The second is merely a quotation from the *Letter to the Soldiers of Coroticus;* the first and third (or whatever of the latter is genuine) [40] would also seem to have been extracted from longer texts.[41]

Our knowledge of these texts and fragments seems ultimately to be derived from a collection of St. Patrick's letters made at some undeterminable date between the saint's death and the early seventh century.[42]

5. Issued with St. Patrick's sanction, if not necessarily drawn up by him personally, is a set of canons decreed by Patrick and his fellow bishops Auxilius and Iserninus. These canons probably were drawn up after the death of Secundinus (447), and they certainly antedate the death of Auxilius (459). Their substantial authenticity [43] is borne out by the fact that the legislators contemplate a state of affairs as might be expected in a Christian community at the very beginning of its existence.

A single canon in the *Book of Armagh* (fol. 21 v, b), decreeing that all controversial matters should be brought before the see of Armagh, from which there was to be an appeal only to the Apostolic See of Rome, is far more problematical. The signatories are Auxilius, Patricius, Secundinus, Benignus. First of all, we miss the name of Iserninus, who, according to the Irish Annals, survived all the four. The second difficulty is that Benignus, Patrick's successor as archbishop of Armagh, signs along with his predecessor.[44] The gravest doubt, however, arises out of the signature of Secundinus (d. 447). The canon can be genuine only if the foundation of Armagh falls within Secundinus' lifetime, which, as we have seen,[45] is far from certain. Inclusion of it in the present collection of texts did not seem justified.

A number of canons in the great Irish collection [46] is attributed to St. Patrick on no authority whatever. The so-called Second Synod of St. Patrick, known only from a *Codex Andegavensis*,[47] is probably a compilation of the seventh century.[48]

As an author St. Patrick can be judged only from the *Confession* and the *Letter to the Soldiers of Coroticus*. The canons are too impersonal; besides, their redactor may have been one of the auxiliary bishops whose names appear along with that of Patrick.

St. Patrick did not regard himself as a man of letters. Of his shortcomings as a writer he was as much aware as any of his critics. More than once he refers to people who hold him in contempt because of his " rusticity," that is, his lack of elegant diction, and frankly admits the truth of the charge (*Conf.* 1, 9–12, 46, 62; *Epist.* 1). Considered

from the point of grammatical correctness, his Latin is
scarcely inferior to the lower stratum of fifth-century
Church Latin, which was already approaching the stage
known as Romance. The impression of poor writing is
due especially to the very marked limitations of his vocab-
ulary and phraseology, the clumsiness of his periods, his
frequent anacolutha, and a general lack of clarity and pre-
cision. At times he is so brief as to become obscure, at
other times he is pedantically explicit. His ideas seldom
develop straightforward, but rather in a meandering way.
His phraseology is largely Biblical, but often a Biblical
phrase takes on a strange meaning in an unusual context.
The two short texts that have survived complete are full
of set phrases and formulas repeated over and over. All
the more striking is the author's powerful personality. In
his defective medium of expression Patrick has given the
world two spiritual and human documents of a strong and
lasting appeal.

The "rusticity" of which Patrick accuses himself
should not be understood too literally. It would certainly
be a gross exaggeration to say that he knew no other book
than the Bible. There is some evidence of his acquaint-
ance with the writings of Sts. Cyprian and Augustine.
He was, of course, familiar with the ecclesiastical legislation of his day. He was also aware of certain demands of
literary form. Both *Confession* and *Epistle* follow a
definite structural pattern: self-introduction of the author;
the argument, culminating in a cluster of Biblical quotations which bear out his case; a formal conclusion, followed by a postscript and a second conclusion. In the
Confession the climax (the Biblical proof) coincides approximately with the point where Patrick turns from his

earlier life to his Irish mission. Even in matters of style Patrick does not betray altogether the literary conventions of antiquity. If in the *Letter* the literary particles *atque* and *ob* are far more frequent, and the word-order is far more conservative than in the *Confession*, the author obviously wanted to satisfy as best he could the literary taste of his addressee or addressees. Similarly, in §§9 and 10 of the *Confession*, where Patrick challenges the *rhetorici*, he employs by way of parody certain elements of rhetorical prose.

*   *   *

In my translation I have endeavoured to retain as much of the flavour of St. Patrick's style as was possible without gross violence to the spirit of the English language. Of earlier translations, only that by Newport J. D. White in *Proceedings of the Royal Irish Academy* 25 C 7 (Dublin 1905) 260–279 is a first-hand translation of a critically established text. My own translation is based on the text of my revised edition in *Classica et Mediaevalia* 11 (Copenhagen 1950) 1–150 (also published as a separate volume by the Irish Manuscripts Commission, Dublin 1952).

In the rendering of New Testament quotations it was possible to use the Challoner version with comparatively little change; in the translation of St. Patrick's Old Testament quotations, which are of decidedly Old Latin character, and of his numerous loose quotations and allusions I had often to attempt a translation of my own. Where Biblical phrases are used with a meaning entirely different from that of the original context, it was sometimes necessary to sacrifice the Biblical flavour to the actual meaning.

The interpretation of certain passages, notably in the *Confession*, is problematical. Readers are urged to consult the notes. I also refer to my commentary on the writings of St. Patrick, *Classica et Mediaevalia* 12 (1951) 79–214 (a reprint by the Irish Manuscripts Commission is in preparation).

Lastly, I wish to make grateful acknowledgment of the permission given me by Messrs. Clonmore & Reynolds, Dublin, to quote freely from my book, *The Life and Legend of St. Patrick* (Dublin, Clonmore & Reynolds, 1949); in particular, to incorporate those sections of St. Patrick's *Confession* which I had already translated in that book.

BIBLIOGRAPHY

SOURCES:

The sources for the life of St. Patrick are, in order of merit:

1. The saint's own writings (see the Introduction, §2).
2. The Irish Annals, especially the *Annals of Ulster* (ed. W. M. Hennessy, Dublin 1887) vol. 1 (Rolls Series), and the *Annals of Innisfallen* (MS British Museum, Rawlinson B. 503; facsimile edition by R. I. Best and E. Mac-Neill, Royal Irish Academy, Dublin 1933; critical edition by S. Mac Airt, Institute for Advanced Studies, Dublin 1951).
3. The *Hymn on St. Patrick* by St. Secundinus (see the present volume, pp. 55–65).
4. The *Life of St. Patrick* by Muirchú and the *Breviarium* of Tírechán, both of the late seventh century, together with other *collectanea* in the *Book of Armagh*

(now in Trinity College, Dublin, MS 52), written *c.* 807.
See the facsimile edition of the Patrician documents in that
manuscript by E. Gwynn (Irish Manuscripts Commission,
Dublin 1937); diplomatic edition, with very full introduction, by J. Gwynn, *Liber Ardmachanus* (Dublin
1913); text edition by E. Hogan, in *Analecta Bollandiana*
1 (1882) 545–85; 2 (1883) 35–68, 213–38; cf. P. Grosjean, "Analyse du Livre d'Armagh," *Anal. Boll.* 42
(1944) 33–41. A new critical edition is being prepared
by the present translator.

　　5. The Irish hymn *Genair Pátraic*, in its present form of
c. 800 A.D.; edited by J. H. Bernard and R. Atkinson,
The Irish Liber Hymnorum, vol. 1, 97–103; English
translation, vol. 2, 31–35: Henry Bradshaw Society, vols.
13 and 14 (London 1898).

　　6. The later Lives of St. Patrick, both in Latin and in
Irish. Of special interest is *Bethu Phátraic*, Colgan's *Tripartite Life*, ed. by K. Mulchrone (Royal Irish Academy,
Dublin 1939); earlier edition, with translation, copious
introduction, and supplementary matters, by W. Stokes,
The Tripartite Life of Patrick, 2 vols. (Rolls Series, London 1887). These Lives are of a predominantly legendary
character, and so are the later Irish traditions about St.
Patrick.

MODERN EDITIONS AND STUDIES:

　　The first critical edition of St. Patrick was made by
Newport J. D. White, *Libri Sancti Patricii. The Latin
Writings of St. Patrick. Ed. with introduction, translation,
and notes*, in Proceedings of the Royal Irish Academy 25
C 7 (Dublin 1905) 201–326; minor edition, SPCK, Texts
for Students 4 (London 1918). See now my own edition

of the text, with textual history, Biblical apparatus, grammatical index, and commentary, in *Classica et Mediaevalia* 11 (1950) 1–150, and 12 (1951) 79–214; the text has been published as a separate volume by the Irish Manuscripts Commission (Dublin 1952), which is also preparing a reissue of the commentary as vol. 2.

Modern historical studies on St. Patrick begin with J. B. Bury, *The Life of St. Patrick and his Place in History* (London 1905). Important are the introductory chapters in J. Gwynn's diplomatic edition of *Liber Ardmachanus* (Dublin 1913). Written for the general reader, but on a scholarly basis, was E. MacNeill, *St. Patrick, Apostle of Ireland* (London 1934). Similar in scope is L. Bieler, *The Life and Legend of St. Patrick* (Dublin 1949). Fundamental is J.F.Kenney, *Sources for the Early History of Ireland.* 1. *Ecclesiastical* (New York 1929) 319–56; add now L. Bieler, *Codices Patriciani Latini. A Descriptive Catalogue of MSS relating to St. Patrick* (Institute for Advanced Studies, Dublin 1942); "Addenda et Corrigenda," *Anal. Boll.* 63 (1945) 242–56; P. Grosjean, "Analyse du Livre d'Armagh," *Anal. Boll.* 62 (1944) 33–41. For a brief survey, consult F. Wotke's article "Patricius" in Pauly-Wissowa-Kroll's *Realenzyklopädie*, vol. 18.2.2 (1949) 2233–41, and my own article, "Patrick, Saint," in *Chamber's Encyclopaedia* 10 (1950) 484 f.

Among general articles I mention M. Tierney, "The European Background of St. Patrick's Mission," *Studies* 21 (1932) 199–212; J. F. Kenney, "St. Patrick and the Patrick Legend," *Thought* 8 (1933) 1–34, 213–29; L. Bieler, "St. Patrick and the Irish People," *Review of Politics* 10 (1948) 290–309; P. Grosjean, "Notes d'hagiographie celtique," *Anal. Boll.* 63 (1945) 65–119; D. S. Nerney, "A Study of St. Patrick's Sources," *Irish Eccles. Record,* 5. ser., 71 (1949) 497–507; 72 (1949) 14–26, 97–110, 259–80.

An ingenious theory was set forth by T. F. O'Rahilly, *The Two Patricks. A Lecture on the History of Christianity in Fifth-Century Ireland* (Institute for Advanced Studies, Dublin 1942); see the same author's *Early Irish History and Mythology* (Institute for Advanced Studies, Dublin 1946) 235–59. According to Prof. O'Rahilly, the author of the *Confession* came to Ireland as late as 460 and died *c.* 491; the Patrick who landed there in 432 and died in 461 was no other than Palladius, who, to believe a note in the *Book of Armagh* (fol. 16 r, a), was surnamed Patricius. This theory has aroused much discussion — see the contributions by G. Murphy, J. Ryan, F. Shaw, and L. Bieler in *Studies* 32 (1943) 297–326; L. Bieler, "The Mission of Palladius," *Traditio* 6 (1948) 1–32.

THE LETTERS OF THE HOLY BISHOP PATRICK

BOOK ONE

CONFESSION [1]

I am Patrick, a sinner, most unlearned, the least of all the faithful, and utterly despised by many. My father was Calpornius, a deacon, son of Potitus, a priest,[2] of the village Bannavem Taburniae;[3] he had a country seat nearby, and there I was taken captive.

I was then about sixteen years of age. I did not know the true God.[4] I was taken into captivity to Ireland with many thousands of people — and deservedly so, because we turned away from God,[5] and did not keep His commandments,[6] and did not obey our priests, who used to remind us of our salvation. And the Lord *brought over us the wrath of His anger*[7] *and scattered us among many nations,*[8] even *unto the utmost part of the earth,*[9] where now my littleness is placed among strangers.

2. And there *the Lord opened the sense of my unbelief*[10] that I might at last remember my sins and *be converted with all my heart to the Lord my God,*[11] who *had regard for my abjection,*[12] and mercy on my youth and ignorance, and watched over me before I knew Him, and before I was able to distinguish between good and evil, and guarded me, and comforted me as would a father his son.

3. Hence I cannot be silent — *nor, indeed, is it expedient*[13] — about the great benefits and the great grace which the Lord has deigned to bestow upon me *in the land*

of my captivity; [14] for this we can give to God in return after having been chastened by Him, *to exalt and praise His wonders* before *every nation that is* anywhere *under the heaven.* [15]

4. Because there is no other God, nor ever was, nor will be, than God the Father unbegotten, without beginning, from whom is all beginning, the Lord of the universe, as we have been taught; and His son Jesus Christ, whom we declare to have always been with the Father, spiritually and ineffably begotten by the Father before the beginning of the world, before all beginning; and by Him are made all things visible and invisible. He was made man, and, having defeated death, was received into heaven by the Father; *and He hath given Him all power over all names in heaven, on earth, and under the earth, and every tongue shall confess to Him that Jesus Christ is Lord and God,* [16] in whom we believe, and whose advent we expect soon to be, *judge of the living and of the dead,* [17] who will render to every man according to his deeds; [18] and *He has poured forth upon us abundantly the Holy Spirit,* [19] *the gift* and *pledge* [20] of immortality, who makes those who believe and obey *sons of God* and *joint heirs with Christ;* [21] and Him do we confess and adore, one God in the Trinity of the Holy Name. [22]

5. For He Himself has said through the Prophet: *Call upon me in the day of thy trouble, and I will deliver thee, and thou shalt glorify me.* [23] And again He says: *It is honourable to reveal and confess the works of God.* [24]

6. Although I am imperfect in many things, I nevertheless wish that my brethren and kinsmen should know what sort of person I am, so that they may understand my heart's desire,

7. I know well *the testimony of my Lord*,[25] who in the Psalm declares: *Thou wilt destroy them that speak a lie.*[26] And again He says: *The mouth that belieth killeth the soul.*[27] And the same Lord says in the Gospel: *Every idle word that men shall speak, they shall render an account for it on the day of judgment.*[28]

8. And so I should dread exceedingly, *with fear and trembling*,[29] this sentence on that day when no one will be able to escape or hide, but we all, without exception, shall have *to give an account*[30] even of our smallest sins *before the judgment seat of* the Lord *Christ.*[31]

9. For this reason I long had in mind to write, but hesitated until now; I was afraid of exposing myself to the talk of men, because I have not studied like the others, who thoroughly imbibed law and Sacred Scripture,[32] and never had to change from the language of their childhood days,[33] but were able to make it still more perfect. In our case, what I had to say had to be translated into a tongue foreign to me, as can be easily proved from the savour of my writing, which betrays how little instruction and training I have had in the art of words; for, so says Scripture, *by the tongue will be discovered the wise man, and understanding, and knowledge, and the teaching of truth.*[34]

10. But of what help is an excuse, however true, especially if combined with presumption, since now, in my old age, I strive for something that I did not acquire in youth? It was my sins that prevented me from fixing in my mind what before I had barely read through. But who believes me, though I should repeat what I started out with?

As a youth, nay, almost as a boy not able to speak, I was taken captive, before I knew what to pursue and what to avoid. Hence to-day I blush and fear exceedingly to reveal my lack of education; for I am unable to tell my story to those versed in the art of concise writing — in such a way, I mean, as my spirit and mind long to do, and so that the sense of my words expresses what I feel.[35]

11. But if indeed it had been given to me as it was given to others, then I would not be silent *because of my desire of thanksgiving;* [36] and if perhaps some people think me arrogant for doing so in spite of my lack of knowledge and my slow tongue, it is, after all, written: *The stammering tongues shall quickly learn to speak peace.*[37]

How much more should we earnestly strive to do this, we, who are, so Scripture says, *a letter of Christ for salvation unto the utmost part of the earth,*[38] and, though not an eloquent one, yet . . . *written in your hearts, not with ink, but with the spirit of the living God!* [39] And again the Spirit witnesses that *even rusticity was created by the Highest.*[40]

12. Whence I, once rustic, exiled, unlearned, who does not know how to provide for the future, this at least I know most certainly that before I was humiliated I was like a stone lying in the deep mire; and He that is mighty came and in His mercy lifted me up, and raised me aloft, and placed me on the top of the wall. And therefore I ought to cry out aloud and so also render something to the Lord for His great benefits here and in eternity — benefits which the mind of men is unable to appraise.

13. Wherefore, then, be astonished, *ye great and little that fear God,*[41] and you men of letters on your estates,[42] listen and pore over this. Who was it that roused up me, the fool that I am, from the midst of those who in the eyes of men are wise, and expert in law, and powerful in word and in everything? And He inspired me — me, the outcast

of this world — before others, to be the man (if only I could!) who, *with fear and reverence and without blame*,[43] should faithfully serve the people to whom the love of Christ conveyed and gave me for the duration of my life, if I should be worthy; yes indeed, to serve them humbly and sincerely.

14. In the light, therefore, of our faith in the Trinity I must make this choice,[44] regardless of danger I must make known the gift of God and everlasting consolation, without fear and frankly I must spread everywhere the name of God so that after my decease I may leave a bequest to my brethren and sons whom I have baptised in the Lord — so many thousands of people.

15. And I was not worthy, nor was I such that the Lord should grant this to His servant; that after my misfortunes and so great difficulties, after my captivity, after the lapse of so many years, He should give me so great a grace in behalf of that nation — a thing which once, in my youth, I never expected nor thought of.

16. But after I came to Ireland — every day I had to tend sheep, and many times a day I prayed — the love of God and His fear came to me more and more, and my faith was strengthened. And my spirit was moved so that in a single day I would say as many as a hundred prayers, and almost as many in the night, and this even when I was staying in the woods and on the mountain; [45] and I used to get up for prayer before daylight, through snow, through frost, through rain, and I felt no harm, and there was no sloth in me — as I now see, because the spirit within me was then fervent.

17. And there one night I heard in my sleep a voice saying to me: " It is well that you fast, soon you will go to

your own country." And again, after a short while, I heard a voice saying to me: "See, your ship is ready." And it was not near, but at a distance of perhaps two hundred miles, and I had never been there, nor did I know a living soul there; and then I took to flight, and I left the man with whom I had stayed for six years. And I went in the strength of God who directed my way to my good, and I feared nothing until I came to that ship.

18. And the day that I arrived the ship was set afloat, and I said that I was able to pay for my passage with them.[46] But the captain was not pleased, and with indignation he answered harshly: "It is of no use for you to ask us to go along with us." And when I heard this, I left them in order to return to the hut where I was staying. And as I went, I began to pray; and before I had ended my prayer, I heard one of them shouting behind me, "Come, hurry, we shall take you on in good faith; make friends with us in whatever way you like." And so on that day I refused to suck their breasts [47] for fear of God, but rather hoped they would come to the faith of Jesus Christ, because they were pagans. And thus I had my way with them, and we set sail at once.

19. And after three days we reached land, and for twenty-eight days we travelled through deserted country.[48] And they lacked food, and hunger overcame them; [49] and the next day the captain said to me: "Tell me, Christian: you say that your God is great and all-powerful; why, then, do you not pray for us? As you can see, we are suffering from hunger; it is unlikely indeed that we shall ever see a human being again."

I said to them full of confidence: "*Be* truly *converted with all your heart to the Lord my God*,[50] because nothing is impossible for Him, that this day He may send you food on your way until you be satisfied; for He has abundance everywhere." And, with the help of God, so it came to pass: suddenly a herd of pigs appeared on the road before our eyes, and they killed many of them; and there they stopped for two nights and fully recovered their strength, and their hounds received their fill, for many of them had grown weak and were half-dead along the way.[51] And from that day they had plenty of food. They also found wild honey, and offered some of it to me, and one of them said: " This we offer in sacrifice." Thanks be to God, I tasted none of it.[52]

20. That same night, when I was alseep, Satan assailed me violently, a thing I shall remember *as long as I shall be in this body*.[53] And he fell upon me like a huge rock, and I could not stir a limb. But whence came it into my mind, ignorant as I am, to call upon Helias? And meanwhile I saw the sun rise in the sky, and while I was shouting " Helias! Helias! " with all my might, suddenly the splendour of that sun fell on me and immediately freed me of all misery.[54] And I believe that I was sustained by Christ my Lord, and that His Spirit was even then crying out in my behalf, and I hope it will be so *on the day of my tribulation*,[55] as is written in the Gospel: *On that day*, the Lord declares, *it is not you that speak, but the Spirit of your Father that speaketh in you*.[56]

21. And once again, after many years, I fell into captivity.[57] On that first night I stayed with them. I heard a divine message saying to me: " Two months will you be with them." And so it came to pass: on the sixtieth night thereafter *the Lord delivered me out of their hands*.[58]

22. Also on our way [59] God gave us food and fire and

dry weather every day, until, on the tenth day, we met
people. As I said above, we travelled twenty-eight days
through deserted country, and the night that we met
people we had no food left.

23. And again after a few years I was in Britain with
my people, who received me as their son, and sincerely be-
sought me that now at last, having suffered so many hardships, I should not leave them and go elsewhere.

And there I saw in the night the vision of a man, whose
name was Victoricus,[60] coming as it were from Ireland,
with countless letters. And he gave me one of them, and
I read the opening words of the letter, which were, " The
voice of the Irish "; and as I read the beginning of the letter I thought that at the same moment I heard their voice —
they were those beside the Wood of Voclut, which is near
the Western Sea [61] — and thus did they cry out *as with one
mouth*: [62] " We ask thee, boy, come and walk among us
once more."

And I was quite broken in heart, and could read no
further, and so I woke up. Thanks be to God, after many
years the Lord gave to them according to their cry.

24. And another night — whether within me, or beside
me, *I know not, God knoweth* [63] — they called me most
unmistakably with words which I heard but could not
understand, except that at the end of the prayer He spoke
thus: " *He that has laid down His life for thee*,[64] it is He
that speaketh in thee "; and so I awoke full of joy.

25. And again I saw Him praying in me, and I was as it
were within my body, and I heard Him above me, that is,
over *the inward man*,[65] and there He prayed mightily with
groanings. And all the time I was astonished, and won-
dered, and thought with myself who it could be that

prayed in me. But at the end of the prayer He spoke, saying that He was the Spirit; and so I woke up, and remembered the Apostle saying: *The Spirit helpeth the infirmities of our prayer. For we know not what we should pray for as we ought; but the Spirit Himself asketh for us with unspeakable groanings, which cannot be expressed in words;* [66] and again: *The Lord our advocate asketh for us.* [67]

26. And when I was attacked by a number of my seniors who came forth and brought up my sins against my laborious episcopate, [68] on that day indeed was I struck so that I might have fallen now and for eternity; but the Lord graciously spared the stranger and sojourner for His name and came mightily to my help in this affliction. Verily, not slight was the shame and blame that fell upon me! I ask God that *it may not be reckoned to them as sin.* [69]

27. As cause for proceeding against me they found — after thirty years! — a confession I had made before I was a deacon. In the anxiety of my troubled mind I confided to my dearest friend what I had done in my boyhood one day, nay, in one hour, because I was not yet strong. *I know not, God knoweth* [70] — whether I was then fifteen years old; and I did not believe in the living God, nor did I so from my childhood, but lived in death and unbelief until I was severely chastised and really humiliated, by hunger and nakedness, and that daily.

28. On the other hand, I did not go to Ireland of my own accord, not until I had nearly perished; but this was rather for my good, for thus was I purged by the Lord; and He made me fit so that I might be now what was once far from me — that I should care and labour for the

salvation of others, whereas then I did not even care about myself.

29. On that day, then, when I was rejected by those referred to and mentioned above, in that night I saw a vision of the night.[71] There was a writing without honour against my face,[72] and at the same time I heard God's voice saying to me: " We have seen with displeasure the face of Deisignatus " (thus revealing his name).[73] He did not say, " Thou hast seen," but, " We have seen," as if He included Himself, as He sayeth: *He who toucheth you toucheth as it were the apple of my eye.*[74]

30. Therefore *I give Him thanks who hath strengthened me*[75] in everything, as He did not frustrate the journey upon which I had decided, and the work which I had learned from Christ my Lord; but I rather felt after this no little strength, and my trust was proved right before God and men.

31. And so I say boldly, my conscience does not blame me now or in the future: God is my witness that I have not lied in the account which I have given you.

32. But the more am I sorry for my dearest friend that we had to hear what he said. To him I had confided my very soul! And I was told by some of the brethren before that defence — at which I was not present, nor was I in Britain, nor was it suggested by me — that he would stand up for me in my absence. He had even said to me in person: " Look, you should be raised to the rank of bishop! " — of which I was not worthy. But whence did it come to him afterwards that he let me down before all, good and evil, and publicly, in a matter in which he had favoured me before spontaneously and gladly — and not he alone, but the Lord, who *is greater than all?*[76]

33. Enough of this. I must not, however, hide God's gift which He bestowed upon me *in the land of my captivity;* [77] because then I earnestly sought Him, and there I found Him, and He saved me from all evil *because* — so I believe — *of His Spirit that dwelleth* [78] in me. Again, boldly said. But God knows it, had this been said to me by a man, I had perhaps remained silent for the love of Christ.

34. Hence, then, I give unwearied thanks to God, who kept me faithful *in the day of my temptation,* [79] so that to-day I can confidently offer Him my soul as a living sacrifice — to Christ my Lord, who *saved me out of all my troubles.* [80] Thus I can say: " *Who am I, O Lord,* and to what hast Thou called me, Thou who didst assist me with such divine power that to-day *I* constantly *exalt* and magnify Thy name *among the heathens* wherever I may be, and not only in good days but also in tribulations? So indeed I must accept with equanimity whatever befalls me, be it good or evil, and always give thanks to God, who taught me to trust in Him always without hesitation, and who must have heard my prayer so that I, however ignorant I was, *in the last days* [81] dared to undertake such a holy and wonderful work — thus imitating somehow those who, as the Lord once foretold, would preach His Gospel *for a testimony to all nations* before *the end of the world.* [82] So we have seen it, and so it has been fulfilled: indeed, we are witnessses that the Gospel has been preached unto those parts beyond which there lives nobody.

35. Now, it would be tedious to give a detailed account of all my labours or even a part of them. Let me tell you briefly how the merciful God often freed me from slavery and from twelve dangers in which my life was at stake [83]

— not to mention numerous plots, which I cannot express in words; for I do not want to bore my readers. But God is my witness, who knows all things even before they come to pass, as He used to forewarn even me, poor wretch that I am, of many things by a divine message.

36. *How came I by this wisdom,*[84] which was not in me, who neither *knew the number of my days* [85] nor knew what God was? Whence was given to me afterwards the gift so great, so salutary — to know God and to love Him, although at the price of leaving my country and my parents?

37. And many gifts were offered to me in sorrow and tears, and I offended the donors, much against the wishes of some of my seniors; [86] but, guided by God, in no way did I agree with them or acquiesce. It was not grace of my own, but God, who is strong in me and resists them all–as He had done when I came to the people of Ireland to preach the Gospel, and to suffer insult from the unbelievers, *hearing the reproach of my going abroad,*[87] and many persecutions even unto bonds, and to give my free birth for the benefit of others; and, should I be worthy, I am prepared to give even my life without hesitation and most gladly for His name, and it is there that I wish to spend it until I die, if the Lord would grant it to me.

38. For I am very much God's debtor, who gave me such great grace that many people were reborn in God through me and afterwards confirmed,[88] and that clerics were ordained for them everywhere, for a people just coming to the faith, whom the Lord took from the utmost parts of the earth, as He once had promised through His prophets: *To Thee the gentiles shall come from the ends of the earth and shall say: " How false are the idols that*

our fathers got for themselves, and there is no profit in them"; and again: *I have set Thee as a light among the gentiles, that Thou mayest be for salvation unto the utmost part of the earth.*[89]

39. And there I wish to wait for His promise who surely never deceives, as He promises in the Gospel: *They shall come from the east and the west, and shall sit down with Abraham and Isaac and Jacob*[90] — as we believe the faithful will come from all the world.

40. For that reason, therefore, we ought to fish well and diligently, as the Lord exhorts in advance and teaches, saying: *Come ye after me, and I will make you to be fishers of men.*[91]   And again He says through the prophets: *Behold, I send many fishers and hunters, saith God,* and so on.[92]   Hence it was most necessary to spread our nets so that a great multitude and throng might be caught for God, and that there be clerics everywhere to baptise and exhort a people in need and want, as the Lord in the Gospel states, exhorts, and teaches, saying: *Going therefore now, teach ye all nations, baptising them in the name of the Father, and the Son, and the Holy Spirit, teaching them to observe all things whatsoever I have commanded you: and behold I am with you all days even to the consummation of the world.*[93]   And again He says: *Go ye therefore into the whole world, and preach the Gospel to every creature. He that believeth and is baptised shall be saved; but he that believeth not shall be condemned.*[94] And again: *This Gospel of the kingdom shall be preached in the whole world for a testimony to all nations, and then shall come the end.*[95]   And so too the Lord announces through the prophet, and says: *And it shall come to pass, in the last days, saith the Lord, I will pour out of my Spirit*

*upon all flesh; and your sons and your daughters shall
prophesy, and your young men shall see visions, and your
old men shall dream dreams.* And upon my servants indeed, and upon my handmaids will I pour out in those days
of my Spirit, and they shall prophesy.[96] And in Osee He
saith: "I will call that which was not my people, my
people; . . . and her that had not obtained mercy, one
that hath obtained mercy. And it shall be in the place
where it was said: 'You are not my people,' there they
shall be called the sons of the living God." [97]

41. Hence, how did it come to pass in Ireland that those
who never had a knowledge of God, but until now always
worshipped idols and things impure, have now been made
a people of the Lord, and are called sons of God, that the
sons and daughters of the kings of the Irish are seen to be
monks and virgins of Christ?

42. Among others, a blessed Irishwoman of noble birth,
beautiful, full-grown, whom I had baptised, came to us
after some days for a particular reason: she told us that she
had received a message from a messenger of God,[98] and he
admonished her to be a virgin of Christ and draw near to
God. Thanks be to God, on the sixth day after this she
most laudably and eagerly chose what all virgins of Christ
do. Not that their fathers agree with them; no — they
often even suffer persecution and undeserved reproaches
from their parents; and yet their number is ever increasing.[99] How many have been reborn there so as to be
of our kind, I do not know — not to mention widows and
those who practice continence.[100]

But greatest is the suffering of those women who live in
slavery. All the time they have to endure terror and
threats. But the Lord gave His grace to many of His

maidens; for, though they are forbidden to do so, they follow Him bravely.

43. Wherefore, then, even if I wished to leave them
and go to Britain — and how I would have loved to go to
my country and my parents, and also to Gaul in order to
visit the brethren and to see the face of the saints of my
Lord! [101]   God knows it that I much desired it; but I am
bound by the Spirit, who gives evidence against me if I do
this, telling me that I shall be guilty; and I am afraid of
losing the labour which I have begun — nay, not I, but
Christ the Lord who bade me come here and stay with
them for the rest of my life, if the Lord will, and will
guard me from every evil way that I may not sin before
Him.

44. This, I presume, I ought to do, but I do not trust
myself *as long as I am in this body of death,*[102] for strong
is he who daily strives to turn me away from the faith and
the purity of true religion to which I have devoted myself
to the end of my life to Christ my Lord. But the hostile
flesh is ever dragging us unto death, that is, towards the
forbidden satisfaction of one's desires; and I know that in
part I did not lead a perfect life as did the other faithful;
but I acknowledge it to my Lord, and do not blush before
Him, because I lie not: from the time I came to know Him
in my youth, the love of God and the fear of Him have
grown in me, and up to now, thanks to the grace of God,
I have kept the faith.

45. And let those who will, laugh and scorn — I shall
not be silent; nor shall I hide the signs and wonders which
the Lord has shown me many years before they came to
pass, as He knows everything even *before the times of the
world.*[103]

46. Hence I ought unceasingly to give thanks to God who often pardoned my folly and my carelessness, and on more than one occasion spared His great wrath on me, who was chosen to be His helper and who was slow to do as was shown me and as the Spirit suggested.[104]   And the Lord had mercy on me thousands and thousands of times because He saw that I was ready, but that I did not know what to do in the circumstances.   For many tried to prevent this my mission; they would even talk to each other behind my back and say: "Why does this fellow throw himself into danger among enemies who have no knowledge of God?"   It was not malice, but it did not appeal to them because — and to this I own myself — of my rusticity.   And I did not realise at once the grace that was then in me; now I understand that I should have done so before.

47. Now I have given a simple account to my brethren and fellow servants [105] who have believed me because of what I said and still say in order to strengthen and confirm your faith.   Would that you, too, would strive for greater things and do better!   This will be my glory, for *a wise son is the glory of his father*.[106]

48. You know, and so does God, how I have lived among you from my youth in the true faith and in sincerity of heart.   Likewise, as regards the heathen among whom I live, I have been faithful to them, and so I shall be.   God knows it, I have overreached none of them, nor would I think of doing so, for the sake of God and His Church, for fear of raising persecution against them and all of us, and for fear that through me the name of the Lord be blasphemed; for it is written: *Woe to the man through whom the name of the Lord is blasphemed*.[107]

49. *For although I be rude in all things,*[108] nevertheless I

have tried somehow to keep myself safe, and that, too, for my Christian brethren, and the virgins of Christ,[109] and the pious women who of their own accord made me gifts and laid on the altar some of their ornaments; and I gave them back to them, and they were offended that I did so. But I did it for the hope of lasting success — in order to preserve myself cautiously in everything so that they might not seize upon me or the ministry of my service, under the pretext of dishonesty, and that I would not even in the smallest matter give the infidels an opportunity to defame or defile.

50. When I baptised so many thousands of people, did I perhaps expect from any of them as much as half a screpall? [110] *Tell me, and I will restore it to you.*[111] Or when the Lord ordained clerics everywhere through my unworthy person and I conferred the ministry upon them free, if I asked any of them as much as the price of my shoes, *speak against me and I will return it to you.*[112]

51. On the contrary, I spent money for you that they might receive me; [113] and I went to you and everywhere for your sake in many dangers, even to the farthest districts, beyond which there lived nobody and where nobody had ever come to baptise, or to ordain clergy, or to confirm the people. With the grace of the Lord, I did everything lovingly and gladly for your salvation.

52. All the while I used to give presents to the kings, besides the fees I paid to their sons who travel with me.[114] Even so they laid hands on me and my companions, and on that day they eagerly wished to kill me; but my time had not yet come. And everything they found with us they took away, and me they put in irons; and on the fourteenth day the Lord delivered me from their power, and

our belongings were returned to us because of God and our dear friends whom we had seen before.[115]

53. You know how much I paid to those who administered justice [116] in all those districts to which I came frequently. I think I distributed among them not less than the price of fifteen men, so that you might enjoy me, and I might always enjoy you in God. I am not sorry for it — indeed it is not enough for me; I still spend and shall spend more. God has power to grant me afterwards *that I myself may be spent for your souls.*[117]

54. Indeed, *I call God to witness upon my soul that I lie not;* [118] neither, I hope, am I writing to you in order to make this an occasion of flattery or covetousness, nor because I look for honour from any of you. Sufficient is the honour that is not yet seen but is anticipated in the heart. *Faithful is He that promised; He never lieth.*[119]

55. But I see myself exalted even in the present world beyond measure by the Lord, and I was not worthy nor such that He should grant me this. I know perfectly well, though not by my own judgment, that poverty and misfortune becomes me better than riches and pleasures. For Christ the Lord, too, was poor for our sakes; and I, unhappy wretch that I am, have no wealth even if I wished for it. Daily I expect murder, fraud, or captivity, or whatever it may be; *but I fear none of these things* [120] because of the promises of heaven. I have cast myself into the hands of God Almighty, who rules everywhere, as the prophet says: *Cast thy thought upon God, and He shall sustain thee.*[121]

56. So, now *I commend my soul to my faithful* [122] God, *for whom I am an ambassador* [123] in all my wretchedness; but God *accepteth no person,*[124] and chose me for this

office — to be, although among His least, one of His ministers.

57. Hence let me *render unto Him for all He has done to me.*[125] But what can I say or what can I promise to my Lord, as I can do nothing that He has not given me? May He *search the hearts and reins;*[126] for greatly and exceedingly do I wish, and ready I was, that He should give me His chalice to drink, as He gave it also to the others who loved Him.

58. Wherefore may God never permit it to happen to me that I should lose His people which He purchased in the utmost parts of the world. I pray to God to give me perseverance and to deign that I be a faithful witness to Him to the end of my life for my God.

59. And if ever I have done any good for my God whom I love, I beg Him to grant me that I may shed my blood with those exiles and captives for His name, even though I should be denied a grave, or my body be woefully torn to pieces limb by limb by hounds or wild beasts, or the fowls of the air devour it. I am firmly convinced that if this should happen to me, I would have gained my soul together with my body, because on that day without doubt we shall rise in the brightness of the sun, that is, in the glory of Christ Jesus our Redeemer,[127] as sons of the living God and *joint heirs with Christ,*[128] *to be made conformable to His image;*[129] for *of Him, and by Him, and in Him*[130] we shall reign.

60. For this sun which we see rises daily for us because He commands so, but it will never reign, nor will its splendour last; what is more, those wretches who adore it will be miserably punished. Not so we, who believe in, and worship, the true sun — Christ — who will never

perish, nor will he *who doeth His will;* but he *will abide for ever as Christ abideth for ever,*[131] who reigns with God the Father Almighty and the Holy Spirit before time, and now, and in all eternity. Amen.

61. Behold, again and again would I set forth the words of my confession. *I testify* in truth and in joy of heart *before God and His holy angels* [132] that I never had any reason except the Gospel and its promises why I should ever return to the people from whom once before I barely escaped.

62. I pray those who believe and fear God, whosoever deigns to look at or receive this writing which Patrick, a sinner, unlearned, has composed in Ireland, that no one should ever say that it was my ignorance if I did or showed forth anything however small according to God's good pleasure; but let this be your conclusion and let it so be thought, that — as is the perfect truth — it was the gift of God. This is my confession before I die.[133]

BOOK TWO

LETTER TO THE SOLDIERS OF COROTICUS [1]

I, Patrick, a sinner, unlearned, resident in Ireland, declare myself to be a bishop. Most assuredly I believe that what I am I have received from God. And so I live among barbarians, a stranger and exile for the love of God. He is witness that this is so. Not that I wished my mouth to utter anything so hard and harsh; but I am forced by the zeal for God; and the truth of Christ has wrung it from me, out of love for my neighbours and sons for whom I gave up my country and parents and *my life to the point of death.*[2] If I be worthy, I live for my God to teach the heathen, even though some may despise me.

2. With my own hand I have written and composed these words, to be given, delivered, and sent to the soldiers of Coroticus; I do not say, to my fellow citizens, or to fellow citizens of the holy Romans,[3] but to fellow citizens of the demons, because of their evil works. Like our enemies, they live in death, allies of the Scots and the apostate Picts.[4] Dripping with blood, they welter in the blood of innocent Christians, whom I have begotten into the number for God [5] and confirmed in Christ!

3. The day after the newly baptised, anointed with chrism, in white garments (had been slain) — the fragrance was still on their foreheads when they were butchered and slaughtered with the sword by the above-mentioned people — I sent a letter with a holy presbyter whom I had taught from his childhood, clerics accompanying him, ask-

ing them to let us have some of the booty, and of the baptised they had made captives. They only jeered at them.

4. Hence I do not know what to lament more: those who have been slain, or those whom they have taken captive, or those whom the devil [6] has mightily ensnared. Together with him they will be slaves in Hell in an eternal punishment; for *who committeth sin is a slave* and will be called *a son of the devil.*[7]

5. Wherefore let every God-fearing man know that they are enemies of me and of Christ my God, *for whom I am an ambassador.*[8] Parricide! fratricide! *ravening wolves that eat the people of the Lord as they eat bread!*[9] As is said, *The wicked, O Lord, have destroyed Thy law,*[10] which but recently He had excellently and kindly planted in Ireland, and which had established itself by the grace of God.

6. I make no false claim. I share in the work of those *whom He called and predestinated* to preach the Gospel amidst grave persecutions *unto the end of the earth,*[11] even if the enemy shows his jealousy through the tyranny of Coroticus, a man who has no respect for God nor for His priests whom He chose, giving them the highest, divine, and sublime power,[12] that *whom they should bind upon earth should be bound also in heaven.*[13]

7. Wherefore, then, I plead with you earnestly, *ye holy and humble of heart,*[14] it is not permissible to court the favour of such people, nor to take food or drink with them, nor even to accept their alms,[15] until they make reparation to God in hardships,[16] through penance, with shedding of tears, and set free the baptised servants of God

and handmaids of Christ, for whom He died and was crucified.

8. *The most High disapproveth the gifts of the wicked. . . . He that offereth sacrifice of the goods of the poor, is as one that sacrificeth the son in the presence of his father.*[17] *The riches,* it is written, *which he has gathered unjustly, shall be vomited up from his belly; the angel of death drags him away, by the fury of dragons he shall be tormented, the viper's tongue shall kill him, unquenchable fire devoureth him.*[18] And so — *Woe to those who fill themselves with what is not their own;* [19] or, *What doth it profit a man that he gain the whole world, and suffer the loss of his own soul?* [20]

9. It would be too tedious to discuss and set forth everything in detail, to gather from the whole Law testimonies against such greed. Avarice is a deadly sin.[21] *Thou shalt not covet thy neighbour's goods. Thou shalt not kill.*[22] A murderer cannot be with Christ. *Whosoever hateth his brother* is accounted *a murderer.*[23] Or, *He that loveth not his brother abideth in death.*[24] How much more guilty is he that has stained his hands with the blood of the sons of God whom He has of late purchased in the *utmost part of the earth* [25] through the call of our littleness!

10. Did I come to Ireland without God, or according to the flesh? Who compelled me? I am bound by the Spirit not to see any of my kinsfolk. Is it of my own doing that I have holy mercy on the people who once took me captive and made away with the servants and maids of my father's house? I was freeborn according to the flesh. I am the son of a decurion.[26] But I sold my noble rank — I am neither ashamed nor sorry — for the good of others.

Thus I am a servant in Christ to a foreign nation for the unspeakable glory *of life everlasting which is in Christ Jesus our Lord.*[27]

11. And if my own people do not know me, *a prophet hath no honour in his own country.*[28] Perhaps we are not of *the same fold* [29] and have not *one and the same God as father,*[30] as is written: *He that is not with me, is against me, and he that gathereth not with me, scattereth.*[31] It is not right that *one destroyeth, another buildeth up.*[32] *I seek not the things that are mine.*[33]

It is not my grace, but God *who has given this solicitude into my heart,*[34] to be one of His hunters or fishers whom God once foretold would come in the last days.[35]

12. I am hated. What shall I do, Lord? I am most despised. Look, Thy sheep around me are torn to pieces and driven away, and that by those robbers, by the orders of the hostile-minded Coroticus. Far from the love of God is a man who hands over Christians to the Picts and Scots. *Ravening wolves* [36] have devoured the flock of the Lord, which in Ireland was indeed growing splendidly with the greatest care; and the sons and daughters of kings were monks and virgins of Christ — I cannot count their number. Wherefore, *be not pleased with the wrong done to the just; even to hell it shall not please.*[37]

13. Who of the saints would not shudder to be merry with such persons or to enjoy a meal with them? They have filled their houses with the spoils of dead Christians, they live on plunder. They do not know, the wretches, that what they offer their friends and sons as food is deadly poison, just as Eve did not understand that it was death she gave to her husband. So are all that do evil: they work death as their eternal punishment.

14. This is the custom of the Roman Christians of Gaul: they send holy and able men to the Franks and other heathen with so many thousand *solidi* to ransom baptised captives.[38] You prefer to kill and sell them to a foreign nation that has no knowledge of God. You betray the members of Christ as it were into a brothel. What hope have you in God, or anyone who thinks as you do, or converses with you in words of flattery? God will judge. For Scripture says: *Not only they that do evil are worthy to be condemned, but they also that consent to them.*[39]

15. I do not know what I should say or speak further about the departed ones of the sons of God, whom the sword has touched all too harshly. For Scripture says: *Weep with them that weep;* [40] and again: *If one member be grieved, let all members grieve with it.*[41] Hence the Church mourns and laments her sons and daughters whom the sword has not yet slain, but who were removed and carried off to faraway lands, where sin abounds openly, grossly, impudently. There people who were freeborn have been sold, Christians made slaves, and that, too, in the service of the abominable, wicked, and apostate Picts! [42]

16. Therefore I shall raise my voice in sadness and grief: [43] O you fair and beloved brethren and sons whom I have begotten in Christ, countless of number, what can I do for you? I am not worthy to come to the help of God or men. *The wickedness of the wicked hath prevailed over us.*[44] *We have been made*, as it were, *strangers.*[45] Perhaps they do not believe that we have received one and the same baptism, or have one and the same God as father. For them it is a disgrace that we are Irish. *Have ye not, as is written, one God? Have ye, every one of you, forsaken his neighbour?* [46]

17. Therefore I grieve for you, I grieve, my dearly beloved. But again, I rejoice within myself. I have not laboured for nothing, and my journeying abroad has not been in vain. And if this horrible, unspeakable crime did happen — thanks be to God, you have left the world and have gone to Paradise as baptised faithful. I see you: you have begun to journey where *night shall be no more, nor mourning, nor death;* [47] *but you shall leap like calves loosened from their bonds, and you shall tread down the wicked, and they shall be ashes under your feet.* [48]

18. You, then, will reign with the apostles, and prophets, and martyrs. [49] You will take possession of eternal kingdoms, as He Himself testifies, saying: *They shall come from the east and from the west, and shall sit down with Abraham, and Isaac, and Jacob in the kingdom of heaven.* [50] *Without are dogs, and sorcerers, . . . and murderers;* [51] *and liars* and perjurers have *their portion in the pool of everlasting fire.* [52] Not without reason does the Apostle say: *Where the just man shall scarcely be saved, where shall the sinner and ungodly transgressor of the law find himself?* [53]

19. Where, then, will Coroticus with his criminals, rebels against Christ, where will they see themselves, they who distribute baptised women as prizes — for a miserable temporal kingdom, which will pass away in a moment? *As a cloud or smoke that is dispersed by the wind, so shall the* deceitful *wicked perish at the presence of the Lord; but the just shall feast with great constancy* with Christ, *they shall judge nations,* [54] and rule over wicked kings for ever and ever. Amen.

20. *I testify before God and His angels* [55] that it will be so as He indicated to my ignorance. It is not my words

that I have set forth in Latin, but those of God and the apostles and prophets, who have never lied. *He that believeth shall be saved; but he that believeth not shall be condemned,*[56] *God hath spoken.*[57]

21. I ask earnestly that whoever is a willing servant of God be a carrier of this letter, so that on no account it be suppressed or hidden by anyone, but rather be read before all the people, and in the presence of Coroticus himself. May God inspire them sometime to recover their senses for God, repenting, however late, their heinous deeds — murderers of the brethren of the Lord! — and to set free the baptised women whom they took captive, in order that they may deserve to live to God, and be made whole, here and in eternity! Be peace to the Father, and to the Son, and to the Holy Spirit. Amen.[58]

FRAGMENTS

I

I heard some (voices) singing psalms in me, and I do not know who they were.[1]

2

(*Book of Armagh:*)[2] Caetiacus and Sacellus ordained bishops, priests, deacons, and other clerics without consulting Patrick in Mag Ái.[3] And Patrick accused them and sent a letter to them, and in repentance they went out to Armagh to Patrick and did the penance of monks, two willing boys of Patrick.[4] And he said to them: "Your churches will not be big."

(Parallel version in *MS Cotton Otho E. XIII:*) In the books of Patrick:[5] The two bishops, Cechianus and Conall, ordained unworthy bishops in Mag Ái. Patrick chided them and said: "Why did you ordain bishops without our advice? How unworthy are these before the Lord to be ordained! Therefore your churches shall always be small." And the monks[6] were moved to penance.

SAYINGS OF PATRICK [1]

1

The fear of God I had as my guide through Gaul and Italy and the islands in the Tyrrhene Sea. [2]

2

From the world you have gone to Paradise. Thanks be to God. [3]

3

Church of the Irish, nay, of the Romans, [in order that you be Christians as are the Romans, you must sing in your churches at every hour of prayer that praiseworthy utterance: *Kyrie eleison, Christe eleison*. Let every church that follows me sing *Kyrie eleison, Christe eleison, Deo gratias*]. [4]

CANONS

We give thanks to God the Father, and the Son, and the Holy Spirit. To the priests, deacons, and all the clergy — Patrick, Auxilius, Iserninus, the bishops, greetings.

We deem it better to forewarn the negligent rather than to condemn accomplished deeds; as Solomon says: *It is better to reason than to be wroth.*[2] Copies of our decisions are given below, and begin thus:

1. If a man has collected money for captives in his community on his own, and without permission, he deserves to be excommunicated.

2. Lectors should acquaint themselves with the church in which each is to sing.

3. There should be no vagrant cleric in the community.[3]

4. If a man has obtained permission, and money has been collected, he should not ask for more than is needed.[4]

5. If anything is left over, he should lay it on the bishop's altar, to be given to some needy person.

6. Any cleric, from ostiary to priest, that is seen without a tunic and does not cover the shame and nakedness of his body, and whose hair is not shorn after the Roman custom,[5] and whose wife goes about with her head unveiled,[6] shall be held in contempt by the laity and removed from the Church.

7. Any cleric who, when summoned, out of negligence

fails to appear at the meetings for matins or vespers shall, except he be held under the yoke of servitude, be considered a stranger.[7]

8. If a cleric has given surety for a pagan in whatsoever amount, and it so happens — as well it might — that the pagan by some ruse defaults upon the cleric, the cleric must pay the debt from his own means; but should he contend with him in arms, let him be reckoned to be outside the Church, as he deserves.

9. A monk and a virgin, the one from one place, the other from another, shall not take lodging in the same inn, nor travel in the same carriage from village to village, nor carry on prolonged conversations together.

10. If a man has made an auspicious beginning as a psalmist, and then quits and lets his hair grow,[8] he is to be excluded from the Church, unless he returns to his former status.

11. If any cleric has been excommunicated by someone and some other person receives him, both are to perform the same penance.

12. If a Christian has been excommunicated, not even his alms are to be accepted.

13. Alms offered by pagans are not to be accepted for the Church.

14. A Christian who has committed murder, or committed adultery, or sworn before a druid as the pagans do,[9] shall do a year's penance for each of these crimes; the year of penance completed, he shall present himself, accompanied by witnesses, and then be freed of his obligation by a priest.

15. And he that commits theft shall do penance for half a year; twenty days on bread only; and, if possible, he shall

return the stolen goods; thus shall he be restored [10] to the Church.

16. A Christian who believes that there is such a thing as a vampire,[11] that is to say, a witch, is to be anathematized — anyone who puts a living soul under such a reputation; and he must not be received again into the Church before he has undone by his own word the crime that he has committed, and so does penance with all diligence.

17. A virgin who has made a vow to God to remain chaste and afterwards has taken a spouse in the flesh, shall be excommunicated until she changes her ways; if she converts and dismisses the adulterer, she shall do penance; and afterwards they shall not live in the same house or on the same farm.

18. If a person is excommunicated, he shall not enter the church even on Easter Night, until he pledges himself to a penance.

19. A Christian woman who has taken a man in honourable marriage and afterwards deserts the same and gives herself to an adulterer, she who does this shall be excommunicated.

20. A Christian who, acting like a pagan, fails to pay a debt shall be excommunicated until he pays the debt.

21. A Christian whom someone has wronged [12] and who calls that person to court, and not to the Church, for the case to be tried, he who does this shall be a stranger.[13]

22. If a man has given his daughter to a man in honourable marriage and she loves another, and he connives with her and receives a bride-price,[14] both shall be excluded from the Church.

23. If a priest has built a church, he shall not offer the

holy sacrifice in it before he has his bishop come to consecrate it; for so it is proper.

24. If a newcomer joins a community, he shall not baptise, or offer the holy sacrifice, or consecrate, or build a church, until he receives permission from the bishop. One who looks to laymen for permission shall be a stranger.[15]

25. If gifts are made by pious people on days when the bishop stays in the several churches, they shall, as is the ancient custom, be the bishop's to dispose of as pontifical gifts, either for his own needs or for distribution among the poor — as the bishop himself will decide.

26. But if a cleric contravenes and is caught encroaching on the gifts, he shall be cut off from the Church as one greedy for sordid gain.

27. Any cleric who is a newcomer in a bishop's community is not allowed to baptise, or to offer the holy sacrifice, or to perform any functions; if he does not abide by this, he shall be excommunicated.

28. If a cleric has been excommunicated, he shall say prayer alone, not in the same house with his brethren; nor is he allowed to offer the holy sacrifice or to consecrate until he has corrected himself; if he does otherwise, he shall be doubly punished.

29. If one of the brethren wishes to receive the grace of God, he shall not be baptised before he has kept the forty days' fast.[16]

30. Any bishop who goes from his own parish [17] to another must not presume to ordain unless he has received permission from him who holds jurisdiction in the place; on the Lord's Day he shall offer the holy sacrifice only by arrangement, and be content to comply in this matter.

31. If one of two clerics who happen to be at odds over some matter hires an enemy of the other who has offered to kill him, he is rightly called a murderer; such a cleric is regarded as excommunicated by all righteous people.

32. If a cleric wishes to come to the aid of a captive, he should assist him with his own money; for if he kidnaps him, many clerics will be blamed because of one thief. He who does this shall be excommunicated.

33. A cleric who comes from the Britons without letters, even though he lives in a community, is not allowed to minister.[18]

34. Similarly, if one of our deacons goes away to another parish without consulting his abbot, and without letters, he should not even be given food;[19] and he shall be punished with penance by the priest whom he has disobeyed. Also a monk who goes wandering without consulting his abbot is to be punished.

ST. SECUNDINUS
HYMN ON ST. PATRICK

INTRODUCTION

The hymn *Audite omnes* (" Hear Ye All "), the earliest in the long series of Latin hymns composed in Ireland,[1] since about 800 A.D. has been attributed to St. Secundinus, a contemporary and fellow missionary of St. Patrick.[2]

Of Secundinus nothing is known on good authority except that he was a bishop, that together with Auxilius and Iserninus he joined Patrick in 439, and that he died in his seventy-fifth year in 447.[3] Eleventh-century tradition[4] has it that he was a son of Restitutus " of the Lombards of Letha (that is, Italy) " and of Patrick's sister Darerca. But Darerca is a legendary character; and so we cannot have much confidence in the rest of the tradition either.[5] That he was born and reared on the continent is reasonably certain; it is an almost inevitable inference from the fact that he came to Ireland as a bishop only seven years after Patrick. His name was later Gaelicised to Sechnall; it is at Domnach Sechnaill, now Dunshaughlin, Co. Meath, that is, at his own see, that the scholiast of the Irish *Book of Hymns* — plausibly enough — makes him compose his hymn.[6] The occasion, Secundinus' desire to atone for criticising Patrick that he neglected to preach charity,[7] is, of course, purely legendary. If, as P. Grosjean suggests with great probability,[8] the hymn of Secundinus falls between St. Patrick's *Epistle* and *Confession*, it served a definite purpose in the interest of its hero: it was written in defence of Patrick against those critics whose hostility had been aroused by his demand to excommunicate Coroticus — a prelude, as it were, to Patrick's own apologia.

There is indeed strong internal evidence to suggest that the hymn was composed in Patrick's lifetime. Patrick is always spoken of as being alive, and references to his eternal reward (verses 20, 91, 92) are always in the future tense. The hymn is entirely free of legendary elements and of allusions to the cult of St. Patrick. His praise, however lavishly bestowed on him, is that of an enthusiastic admirer and defender; it has none of the characteristics of *gloria postuma*. A fifth-century date is suggested also by the Old Latin Biblical text of which the author makes use, and by his Latinity and manner of versification.[9]

Audite omnes is an abecedarian hymn, that is to say, its stanzas begin with the consecutive letters of the alphabet. It thus belongs to the same class of poetry as St. Augustine's *Psalmus contra partem Donati*.[10] It differs from the latter in its metrical structure and in that it does not rime. With Augustine's Psalm it has in common that its metre is based on a simple count of syllables (16 per line in Augustine, 15 in Secundinus) and that it was composed with a view to propaganda.

The hymn consists of twenty-three stanzas of four long lines each. The line is a version of the ancient Roman *versus quadratus* (catalectic trochaic tetrameter with *caesura* after the eighth syllable), but without regard for either prosody or accent — except at the end of lines, where the accent is always preserved and an echo of classical prosody can often be heard. Assonance and alliteration are probably intentional where they occur, but are not, as in Gaelic poetry, part of the structural pattern.

As I have not ventured on a verse translation, I quote

here the first stanza in the original in order to give the reader some illustration of the comments just made:

Audite omnes amantes Deum sancta mereta
Viri in Christo beati Patrici episcopi,
Quomodo bonum ob actum similatur angelis
Perfectamque propter vitam aequatur apostolis.

The hymn enjoyed great popularity in Ireland. As early as the seventh century it was included in the Antiphonary of Bangor. About the same time, Muirchú in his *Life of St. Patrick* (2.6) states that shortly before his death Patrick was granted the favour that all persons who sang this hymn on their last day would be saved by his intercession. In Tírechán's files (*Book of Armagh*, fol. 16 r, a) there is a note [11] saying that in honour of St. Patrick "his canticle" should be sung in all Ireland throughout the triduum of his *dormitio* (that is, from the 17th to the 19th of March). In the hymn *Genair Pátraic* (c. 800 A.D.) the hymn of Secundinus is called a protection, that is, a "breast-plate" (*lorica*) or prayer of special power.[12] In order to avail oneself of this protection it was later thought sufficient to recite the last three stanzas only.[13]

The hymn *Audite omnes* is preserved in four mediaeval manuscripts: the Antiphonary of Bangor (680–91), the two eleventh-century copies of the Irish *Liber Hymnorum* (in Trinity College, Dublin, and the Franciscan Library, Killiney, respectively) and in the Leabhar Breac (written before 1411) in the Royal Irish Academy; the last three stanzas only are found in an eleventh-century Exeter manuscript, now at Corpus Christi College, Cambridge.

*　　*　　*

The prose translation offered here is based on my own reconstruction of the text which I hope to publish before long.

BIBLIOGRAPHY

Critical editions: J. H. Bernard and R. Atkinson, *The Irish Liber Hymnorum* 1.7–13; 2.xiii–xiv, 96–106 (Henry Bradshaw Society 13, 14, London 1898); C. Blume, *Analecta hymnica medii aevi* 51 (Leipzig 1908) 340–46.

Commentary: G. F. Hamilton, *In St. Patrick's Praise: the Hymn of St. Secundinus* (Dublin 1920: text [Bernard-Atkinson], introduction, prose and verse translation, copious notes); E. MacNeill, " The Hymn of St. Secundinus in Honour of St. Patrick," *Irish Historical Studies* 2 (1939–40) 129–53. For general discussion consult J. F. Kenny, *Sources for the Early History of Ireland.* 1. *Ecclesiastical* (New York 1929) 258–60.

HYMN ON ST. PATRICK,
TEACHER OF THE IRISH [1]

Hear ye all, lovers of God, the holy merits
Of the man blessed in Christ, Patrick the bishop,
How for his good ways he is likened to the angels,
And because of his perfect life is deemed equal to the
    apostles.

Christ's holy precepts he keeps in all things,
His works shine bright among men,
And they follow his holy and wondrous example,
And thus praise God the Father in heaven.

Constant in the fear of God and steadfast in his faith,
On him the Church is built as on Peter;
And his apostleship has he received from God —
The gates of Hell will not prevail against him. [2]

The Lord has chosen him to teach the barbarian tribes, [3]
To fish with the nets of his teaching,
And to draw from the world unto grace the believers,
Men who would follow the Lord to His heavenly seat.

He sells the choice talents of Christ's Gospel
And collects them among the Irish heathens with usury; [4]
As a reward for the great labour of his journey,
His will be the joy of heaven's kingdom in union with
    Christ.

61

God's faithful servant and His distinguished ambassador,
He gives the good an apostolic example and model,
Preaching as he does to God's people in words as well as
    in deeds,
So that him whom he converts not with words he inspires
    with good conduct.[5]

25   Glory has he with Christ, honour in the world,
He who is venerated by all as an angel of God.[6]
God has sent him, as He sent Paul, an apostle to the
    gentiles,
To offer men guidance to the kingdom of God.

Humble is he of mind and body because of his fear of
    God;
30   The Lord has pleasure in him because of his good deeds;
In his holy body he bears the marks of Christ;[7]
In His Cross alone, his sole comfort, he glories.[8]

Untiringly he feeds the faithful from the heavenly ban-
    quet,
Lest those who are with Christ faint on the way;
35   Like bread he gives to them the words of the Gospel,
Which are multiplied like manna in his hands.[9]

He preserves his body chaste for love of the Lord;
This body he has made a temple for the Holy Spirit,
And he keeps it such by purity in all his actions;
40   He offers it as a living sacrifice, acceptable to the Lord.[10]

The great Gospel light of the world is he,
Lifted up on a candlestick, shining over all the earth —

The fortified city of the King, seated on a mountain,[11]
Wherein there is great abundance of the Lord.

15 Greatest indeed will be called in the kingdom of heaven
The man who fulfils with good deeds the holy words he
    teaches,
Who by his good example is a leader and model to the
    faithful,
Who in sincerity of heart has confidence in God.

Boldly he proclaims the name of the Lord to the heathens,
20 And gives them eternal grace in the bath of salvation.
He prays to God daily for their sins,
For them he offers sacrifices, worthy in the eyes of God.[12]

For the sake of God's law he despises all worldly glory;
Compared to His table he considers all else as trifling;
25 He is not moved by the violence of this world,
But, suffering for Christ, he rejoices in adversity.[13]

A good and faithful shepherd of the flock won for the
    Gospel,
God has chosen him to watch over God's people
And to feed with divine teaching His folk,
30 For whom, following Christ's example, he gives his life.[14]

For his merits the Saviour has raised him to the dignity of a
    bishop,
That he may spur the clergy in their heavenly service,[15]
Providing them with heavenly rations, besides vestments —
The rations of divine and sacred words.[16]

65 He is the King's herald, inviting the faithful to the wed-
ding.
He is richly clad in a wedding garment,[17]
He drinks heavenly wine from heavenly cups
And gives God's people the spiritual cup to drink.[18]

He finds a holy treasure in the Sacred Volume
70 And perceives the Saviour's divinity in His flesh.
It is a treasure he purchases with holy and perfect works.
ISRAEL his soul is called — " seeing God." [19]

A faithful witness of the Lord to the Catholic Law,
His speech is spiced with divine words,
75 That the human flesh may not decay, eaten by worms,
But be salted with heavenly savour for sacrifice.

A true and renowned tiller of the Gospel field,
His seeds are Christ's Gospels.
These he sows from his God-inspired mouth into the ears
of the wise,
80 And cultivates their hearts and minds with the Holy Spirit.

Christ chose him to be His vicar on earth.
He frees captives from a twofold servitude:
The great numbers whom he liberates from bondage to
men,
These countless ones he frees from the yoke of the devil.

85 Hymns, and the Apocalypse, and the Psalms of God he
sings,[20]
And explains them for the edification of God's people.

What he tells them he believes in the Trinity of the holy
    Name,[21]
And teaches that there is only one substance in Three
    Persons.

Girt with the Lord's girdle day and night,
o He prays unceasingly to God the Lord.
He will receive the reward for his immense labour —
With the Apostles will he reign, holy, over Israel.[22]

APPENDIX

THE *LORICA*

INTRODUCTION

The text commonly known as the *Lorica* or *Breast-Plate* of St. Patrick is an Old Irish morning prayer, primarily an invocation of the Holy Trinity, which in its present form most probably dates from the ninth century.[1] Its composition by St. Patrick is a possibility that should not be rashly dismissed. The sentiments expressed as well as certain archaic features in syntax and metre would suggest that the poem is of early (at least sixth-century) date. It may have been handed down orally until, in the ninth century, the form in which it survives was transmitted to writing.[2] The story that by its recitation Patrick made himself and his companions appear as so many deer to the men of Laogaire who lay in ambush for them, is first related in the preface to this piece as found in the Irish *Book of Hymns;* it is at this point that the hymn is inserted in the interpolated version of the Middle Irish *Tripartite Life of Patrick.* In reminiscence of this story the traditional title of the prayer, *Fáeth Fiada,* was interpreted as " the deer's cry "; originally it probably meant " magic mist " — an incantation that was supposed to make a person invisible.[3]

This is one of a number of Irish prayers, called *Loricae,* some in Latin, some in Gaelic, that were credited with the special power of protecting those who would recite them

67

against all sorts of dangers to body and soul.[4] Such prayers replaced pagan charms when the Irish accepted the Christian faith.

Although St. Patrick's authorship cannot be proved, I feel that the *Lorica* should be included in this volume — not only as a text frequently associated with the name of St. Patrick, but also because it is a most beautiful Old Irish prayer which combines a profoundly religious spirit with poetic grandeur.

*　　*　　*

The translation given below is substantially that of W. Stokes and J. Strachan, *Thesaurus Palaeohibernicus* 2 (Cambridge 1903) 354–58 — the most accurate in existence. The slight changes made by the present translator do not affect the sense. Two corrections, in lines 5 (=73) and 64 respectively, are due to E. Knott, *Eriu* 7 (1913–14) 239, and R. Thurneysen, *Zeitschrift für vergleichende Sprachforschung* 31 (1889–91) 97.

I wish to express my thanks to Professors Gerard Murphy, of University College, Dublin, and M. A. O'Brien, Director of the Celtic school in the Dublin Institute for Advanced Studies, who have generously assisted me with their expert knowledge of Old Irish poetry.

PATRICK'S HYMN

Patrick made this hymn. It was made in the time of Loegaire son of Niall.[1] The cause of its composition, however, was to protect him and his monks against deadly enemies that lay in wait for the clerics. And this is a breast-plate of faith for the protection of body and soul against devils and men and vices. When anyone shall repeat it every day with diligent intentness on God, devils shall not dare to face him, it shall be a protection to him against every poison and envy, it shall be a defence to him against sudden death, it shall be a breast-plate to his soul after his death. Patrick sang this hymn when ambuscades were laid against his coming by Loegaire, that he might not go to Tara [2] to sow the faith. And then it appeared before those lying in ambush that they (Patrick and his monks) were wild deer, with a fawn (Benén) [3] following them. And its name is " Deer's Cry."

I arise to-day
   through a mighty strength, the invocation of the
      Trinity,
   through belief in the Threeness,
   through confession of the Oneness
   towards the Creator.

I arise to-day
   through the strength of Christ with His Baptism,
   though the strength of His Crucifixion with His Burial,
   through the strength of His Resurrection with His
      Ascension,
   through the strength of His descent for the Judgment
      of Doom.

I arise to-day
   through the strength of the love of Cherubim,
   in obedience of Angels,
   in the service of the Archangels,
   in hope of resurrection to meet with reward,
   in prayers of Patriarchs,

in predictions of Prophets,
in preachings of Apostles,
in faiths of Confessors,
20   in innocence of Holy Virgins,
in deeds of righteous men.

I arise to-day
through the strength of Heaven:
light of Sun,
25   brilliance of Moon,
splendour of Fire,
speed of Lightning,
swiftness of Wind,
depth of Sea,
30   stability of Earth,
firmness of Rock.

I arise to-day
through God's strength to pilot me:
God's might to uphold me,
35   God's wisdom to guide me,
God's eye to look before me,
God's ear to hear me,
God's word to speak for me,
God's hand to guard me,
40   God's way to lie before me,
God's shield to protect me,
God's host to secure me —
    against snares of devils,
    against temptations of vices,
45   against inclinations (?) of nature,
    against everyone who shall wish me ill,

afar and anear,
alone and in a crowd.

I summon to-day all these powers between me (and these
   evils) —
      against every cruel and merciless power that may
         oppose my body and my soul,
      against incantations of false prophets,
      against black laws of heathenry,
      against false laws of heretics,
      against craft (?) of idolatry,
      against spells of women and smiths [4] and wizards,
      against every knowledge < that endangers > man's
         body and soul.

Christ to protect me to-day
      against poison, against burning,
      against drowning, against wounding,
      so that there may come abundance of reward.
Christ with me, Christ before me, Christ behind me,
Christ in me, Christ beneath me, Christ above me,
Christ on my right, Christ on my left,
Christ where I lie, Christ where I sit, Christ where I arise,
Christ in the heart of every man who thinks of me,
Christ in the mouth of every man who speaks of me,
Christ in every eye that sees me,
Christ in every ear that hears me.

I arise to-day
      through a mighty strength, the invocation of the
         Trinity,
      through belief in the Threeness,

through confession of the Oneness
towards the Creator.

Salvation is of the Lord.
75 Salvation is of the Lord.
Salvation is of Christ.
May Thy salvation, O Lord, be ever with us.[5]

NOTES

LIST OF ABBREVIATIONS

AB	*Analecta Bollandiana*
Bieler	L. Bieler, *The Life and Legend of St. Patrick. Problems of Modern Scholarship* (Dublin 1949)
C & M 11 (12)	*Classica et Mediaevalia* 11 (1950) 1-150: L. Bieler, *Libri Epistolarum Sancti Patricii Episcopi*—Part I, Introduction, Text, Indices; 12 (1951) 79-214: the same—Part II, Commentary
CIL	*Corpus inscriptionum latinarum*
Conf.	St. Patrick's *Confession*
Epist.	St. Patrick's *Epistle* (*Letter to the Soldiers of Coroticus*)
IER	*Irish Ecclesiastical Record*, 5. series
Kenney	James F. Kenney, *The Sources for the Early History of Ireland*. 1. *Ecclesiastical* (New York 1929)
MGH	*Monumenta Germaniae historica*
Muirchú	Muirchú, *Life of St. Patrick* (the division of books and chapters is that of the *Book of Armagh*)

THE WORKS OF ST. PATRICK

INTRODUCTION

[1] The date of Patrick's birth can be approximately calculated on the following basis. On his escape from Ireland to the continent at the age of twenty-two, Patrick and the traders who had taken him aboard travelled twenty-eight days through "desert land" (Conf. 19). It is generally agreed that the country where they landed was Gaul, and that *desertum* refers to the state of this province in or about 407 (see below, n. 11). Patrick's description, however, is too vague for any inference to be cogent. The devastation of Gaul by Attila in 451 would certainly be too late even for the late birth date of St. Patrick (*c.* 420) postulated by T. F. O'Rahilly (see Introd. 20). The search for Patrick's birthplace is quite hopeless. If the description of Patrick's father

75

as *decurio* (Epist. 10) means that the latter was a civil magistrate,
Patrick must have been born in that part of Britain which was
thoroughly Romanized—probably in the south-west, which lay
open to Irish raids.   Among the numerous identifications that
have been attempted, Ravenglass in Cumberland (cf. P. Grosjean,
"La patrie de S. Patrice," AB 63 [1945] 65-72) would be most
acceptable from the geographical and historical point of view.
I doubt, however, that the *Bannauem Taburniae* (or *Taberniae*)
of Conf. 1 could be plausibly claimed as a misreading of the
ancient name of Ravenglass, *Clannaventa Berniciae*.   On the other
hand, *Bannauem Taburniae* need not be Patrick's birthplace.
Patrick merely says that his father had a country house or a
farm near this place, and that he himself was captured there by
Irish raiders.   If, as is just possible, *decurio* designates a man of
military rank, Patrick might have been born in one of the Roman
garrisons farther to the north.

[2] Conf. 1.

[3] Muirchú 1.1.   On what authority this statement is made we
do not know.   A Q. Calpurnius Concessinius is known from an
inscription of Roman Britain (CIL 7.481).   Concessa's blood
relationship with St. Martin of Tours is entirely legendary.

[4] See above, n. 1.

[5] J. B. Bury, *Life of St. Patrick* (London 1905) 19 f.

[6] Conf. 1, and *passim*.

[7] *Ibid.*

[8] Conf. 27.

[9] Conf. 16 f.

[10] Conf. 18 f.

[11] So P. Grosjean in a review of Patriciana, AB 54 (1936) 196-
99.   Other scholars (Bury, MacNeill) have thought of the devastation of Gaul by the Vandals earlier in 407.   E. A. Thompson,
"A Note on St. Patrick in Gaul," *Hermathena* 79 (1952) 22-29,
suggests that there might also have been a revolt of the peasants
in Armorica following the Vandal invasion.

[12] Conf. 23.   There is no reason why *cum parentibus meis*
should not mean "with my parents."   If, as it seems, Patrick was
captured during a sojourn at the old family seat, his parents might
well have stayed at home and thus been spared.

[13] See Conf. 23-25, with references in the notes.

[14] This is not stated explicitly in his own writings.   Muirchú
1.5-9, where the story is given in detail, seems to depend on an

ancient tradition of the church of Auxerre (T. F. O'Rahilly, *The Two Patricks* [Dublin 1942] 19). Two passages in the text of St. Patrick (Conf. 43, Epist. 14), however, and the first "Saying of Patrick" testify to his stay in Gaul. See P. Grosjean, "Notes chronologiques sur le séjour de S. Patrice en Gaule," AB 63 (1945) 73-93.

[15] Conf. 27. It would appear that Patrick was never a presbyter, but was made bishop directly from the diaconate.

[16] Prosper, *Chronicon*, under 429 (MGH, *Chronica minora* ed. T. Mommsen, 1. 473).

[17] Such criticism seems to be alluded to in Conf. 46.

[18] Cf. Conf. 32.

[19] Prosper, *Chronicon*, under 431: "To the Irish believing in Christ, Palladius, ordained by Pope Celestine, is sent as their first bishop."

[20] Muirchú 1. 8 f. See P. Grosjean, "Notes chronologiques . . .," AB 63 (1945) 82-86; L. Bieler, "The Ordination of St. Patrick," *Scriptorium* 2 (1948) 286 f.

[21] According to T. F. O'Rahilly, *Early Irish History and Mythology* (Dublin 1946) 235-59, the several bodies of Irish annals derive their early portions from an Ulster chronicle of the eighth century. The same date 432 is implied, in the preceding century, in a note of Tírechán (*Book of Armagh*, fol. 9 r, b). Beyond this, documentary evidence does not go; but 432 as the date of St. Patrick's arrival in Ireland is favoured by general historical considerations. See P. Grosjean, *loc. cit.*; L. Bieler, "The Mission of Palladius," *Traditio* 6 (1948) 1-32.

[22] Published by A. W. Haddan and W. Stubbs, *Councils and Ecclesiastical Documents relating to Great Britain and Ireland* 2.2 (Oxford 1873) 328-31. English translation, with notes, in J. T. MacNeill and H. M. Gamer, *Medieval Handbooks of Penance* (New York 1938) 75-80; and in this volume, 50-54.

[23] See Annals of Ulster, Annals of Innisfallen, and *Chronicum Scotorum* (Rolls Series) under that year.

[24] The available evidence is presented and discussed by L. Bieler, "St. Patrick and the Irish People," *Review of Politics* 10 (1948) 290-309.

[25] Ancient Ireland was divided into more than a hundred independent small states, which were often at war with each other.

[26] Conf. 41 f.; Epist. 12. Cf. J. Ryan, *Irish Monasticism* (Dublin 1931) 59-96.

[27] See T. F. O'Rahilly, *The Two Patricks* 64 f. The correct date is possibly that given in the Annals of the Four Masters, 457: L. Bieler, "Sidelights on the Chronology of St. Patrick," *Irish Hist. Stud.* 6 (1949) 259 f.

[28] Conf. 35.

[29] Conf. 55, 59.

[30] Cf. S. Malone, *Chapters towards a Life of St. Patrick* (Dublin 1892) 140-93; E. MacNeill, *St. Patrick, Apostle of Ireland* (London 1934) 78; Bieler 89.

[31] But there is no need of supposing that when the *Confession* was written Patrick felt his death approaching. In fact, the *Confession* may have been composed as early as the late forties of the fifth century.

[32] Cf. P. Grosjean, "Quand fut composée la Confession de S. Patrice?" AB 63 (1945) 107; G. Misch, *Geschichte der Autobiographie* 1 (2nd ed. Leipzig 1931) 455; L. Bieler, "The Place of Saint Patrick in Latin Language and Literature," *Vigiliae Christianae* 6 (1952) 69 f.

[33] D. S. Nerney, "A Study of St. Patrick's Sources, I," IER 71 (1949) 499-507.

[34] Conf. 14. On the meaning of *exagellia*, see my note in *Amer. Jour. Philol.* 69 (1948) 309-312; also C & M 12.129.

[35] Epist. 3 reads like the echo of a baptismal rubric; "Saying" 3 (if authentic) refers to the observance of the canonical hours; in the hymn of St. Secundinus (line 85) we hear about Patrick's habit of reciting the Psalter and singing hymns.

[36] D. S. Nerney, "A Study of St. Patrick's Sources, III," IER 72 (1949) 97-110.

[37] See L. Bieler, "Der Bibeltext des heiligen Patrick," *Biblica* 28 (1947) 31-58, 236-63; C. Charlier, *Bulletin d'ancienne littérature chrétienne* 3 (*Revue Bénéd.* 1948) 77.

[38] The later date suggested by T. F. O'Rahilly, *The Two Patricks* 67 f., namely *c.* 480-490, is in itself less probable, and seems to be bound up with Professor O'Rahilly's theory that "Patrick the Briton," author of our texts, died as late as *c.* 490. According to the genealogies in MS. Brit. Mus. Harley 3859, which O'Rahilly invokes as his authority, Ceredig's father Cunedda died *c.* 447.

[39] See the convincing argumentation of P. Grosjean, "Quand fut composée la Confession de S. Patrice?" AB 63 (1945) 100-111; E. MacNeill, "The Hymn of St. Secundinus in Honour of

St. Patrick," *Irish Hist. Stud.* 2.140-43. It would appear, then, that the *Confession* was written not long after the *Epistle*. The hymn of Secundinus with its apologetic tendency seems to be of approximately the same date. The sequence of the three works obviously was: *Letter to the Soldiers of Coroticus—Hymn of Secundinus—Confession:* cf. Bieler 38-40. It was the indignation aroused in British ecclesiastical circles by Patrick's *Letter* that prompted the "defence" of Patrick's mission, first by Secundinus, and then by himself. Secundinus, according to the Annals, died in 447. St. Patrick's *Letter* must have preceded the hymn by at least several months, and the raid of Coroticus took place some time before the *Letter* was written. The raid would thus fall in the very beginning of the reign of Coroticus, Patrick's *Letter* and Secundinus' hymn within a year's time from that event, the *Confession c.* 448.

[40] See below, p. 49.

[41] P. Grosjean, "Notes sur les documents anciens concernant S. Patrice," AB 62 (1944) 50 f.

[42] C & M 11.27-29.

[43] Only canons 25, 30, 33, 34, and a clause in canon 6 are open to the suspicion of having been interpolated; cf. Bury, *op. cit.* 233 ff.; Kenney 169 ff.

[44] This difficulty might be removed on the assumption that Benignus' name was added at a reissue of this canon after Patrick's death: cf. MacNeill, *op. cit.* 74 f.

[45] See p. 96. For the text of the Armagh canon, cf. Haddan and Stubbs (see above, n. 22) 2.2.332.

[46] Cf. H. Wasserschleben, *Die irische Kanonensammlung* (2nd ed. Leipzig 1885).

[47] Cologne, Chapter Library, MS xci. Edited first by H. Spelman in 1639; reprinted by Haddan and Stubbs (see above, n. 22) 2.2.333-38. English translation in MacNeill and Gamer (see n. 22) 75-80.

[48] Cf. Bury, *op. cit.* 339.

TEXT

CONFESSION

[1] The *Confession* is preserved in the manuscript known as the *Book of Armagh*, c. 807 (see above, SOURCES No. 4); both *Con-*

fession and *Letter to the Soldiers of Coroticus* in a number of legendaria, partly Continental, partly English, dating from the tenth to the twelfth century. See L. Bieler, *Codices Patriciani Latini* 1–3; C & M. 11.7–10. The division of Patrick's letters into books is found only in three late MSS, but there is reason for believing that it was introduced by the original collector: C & M 11.28.

[2] Potitus probably became a presbyter or priest when he was advanced in years. See Introd. 3.

[3] Identification remains problematical. See Bieler 51-53, with notes, and above, Introd. n. 1.

[4] This and similar statements later in the text (Conf. 12, 27) must be read in the light of Patrick's "conversion." Nominal Christian though he was, he did not know the "living God" prior to his captivity in Ireland.

[5] Cf. Isa. 59.13; Bar. 3.8; Dan. 9.5; etc.

[6] Cf. Gen. 26.5; Ezech. 44.24; etc.

[7] Isa. 42.25.

[8] Jer. 9.16; Tob. 13.4.

[9] Acts 13.47.

[10] Conflation of Luke 24.45 and Heb. 3.12?

[11] Joel 2.12, 13.

[12] Reminiscence of Luke 1.48?

[13] 2 Cor. 12.1.

[14] Tob. 13.7.

[15] Conflation of Isa. 25.1 (cf. Ps. 88.6) and Acts 2.5 (with reminiscence of Dan. 9.12?).

[16] Phil. 2.9-11.

[17] Acts 10.42.

[18] Rom. 2.6 (cf. Ps. 61.13; Prov. 24.12; Ecclus. 16.15; Matt. 16.27).

[19] Titus 3.5 f.

[20] Cf. Acts 2.38 and Eph. 1.14.

[21] Rom. 8.16 f.

[22] This paragraph is often referred to as St. Patrick's Creed. It is not a formal creed, but rather a motto for his *Confession*— the author wishes us to see his missionary work in the light of his belief in the Holy Trinity (cf. C & M 12.97). From an analysis of the credal formulas here used it is evident that behind Patrick's words there lies the text of some Gallican creed with Eastern affiliations—the same creed that is reflected, independ-

ently, so it seems to me, in Victorinus of Pettau's *Commentary on the Apocalypse* 11.1. See L. Bieler, "The 'Creeds' of St. Victorinus and St. Patrick," *Theol. Stud.* 9 (1948) 121-24. For different views, cf. F.R.M. Hitchcock, "The Creeds of SS. Irenaeus and Patrick," *Hermathena* 14 (1907) 168-82, and J. E. L. Oulton, *The Credal Statements of St. Patrick* (Dublin 1940). No reference to St. Patrick is made in J. N. D. Kelly, *Early Christian Creeds* (London 1950).

[23] Ps. 49.15.

[24] Tob. 12.7.

[25] 2 Tim. 1.18.

[26] Ps. 5.7.

[27] Wisd. 1.11.

[28] Matt. 12.36.

[29] Eph. 6.5; Phil. 2.12.

[30] Rom. 14.12 (or allusion to Matt. 12.36).

[31] 2 Cor. 5.10.

[32] In the late centuries of the Roman Empire the administration of civil law not seldom fell to the bishops; a certain amount of legal knowledge was part of the curriculum in the higher schools of fifth-century Gaul. See T. Haarhoff, *Schools of Gaul* (Oxford 1920) 83, 153; C. F. Stevens, *Sidonius Apollinaris and His Age* (Oxford 1933) 8, 216-21. Patrick probably thinks of the higher clergy in Britain and Gaul. The same persons are obviously understood by *sapientes et legis periti et potentes in sermone*, Conf. 13.

[33] This and the following statement are controversial. Certain it is that Patrick makes a distinction between himself and his compatriots. Unlike the others, he had "to change his language" and was prevented from making steady progress towards a perfect command of it. This is proved, he says, by the fact that in writing his *Confession* he had to translate into a foreign language—hence the "rustic" flavour of his writing. In his youth, at a time when his former schoolmates went on with their study of Latin in the rhetorical schools, he spent his days as a slave in Ireland. He must have learnt some Gaelic there and spoken this language regularly after his return to Ireland as a missionary. N. J. D. White, *Libri Sancti Patricii* 284, has argued that the *lingua aliena* is probably Irish; if so, the words *sermo et loquela nostra translata est in linguam alienam* would be the negative counterpart to *sermones illorum ex infantia numquam mutarunt*.

Although this interpretation has been widely accepted, I doubt its correctness. It seems far more natural to me to understand *translata est* as "has been translated"; on this assumption Patrick speaks not of his language in general, but of the text of his *Confession* (cf. Epist. 20: *quod ego Latinum exposui*). The foreign language *into* which he translates must then be Latin.

But what is the language *from* which he translates? Is it Gaelic? This language was hardly less foreign to Patrick than Latin. I think Patrick's first language, as that of his schoolfellows, was the Celtic of Britain, that is, an early form of Welsh. Latin, which was the official language of the country in so far as it was a Roman province, had to be learnt at school. Only, whereas the others had the benefit of its uninterrupted study and practice, which in course of time made them fluent speakers and writers, for Patrick it always remained "alien." Patrick's words do not necessarily imply that his *Confession* was translated from a draft in some other language, but merely that it was not conceived in Latin in the author's mind.

[34] Ecclus. 4.29. The Biblical text has been slightly modified—unintentionally, I think—by the force of the argument.

[35] *Unde ergo hodie erubesco et vehementer pertimeo denudare imperitiam meam, quia desertis brevitate sermone explicare nequeo, sicut enim spiritus gestit et animus, et sensus monstrat adfectus.*

[36] *Propter retributionem:* Ps. 118.112. In the original context the phrase means "on account of the reward"; here it expresses Patrick's desire to give praise to God in acknowledgment of His favours. Cf. C & M 12.121.

[37] Isa. 32.4 (Septuagint). In *slow tongue* there is an evident allusion to Exod. 4.10.

[38] Cf. 2 Cor. 3.2.

[39] Cf. *ibid.* 3.3. I have not translated the unintelligible words *ratum (et) fortissimum*—remnants, it seems, of an ancient gloss.

[40] Ecclus. 7.16. Patrick seems to have misinterpreted *rusticatio* ("husbandry") as *rusticitas*.

[41] Apoc. 19.5.

[42] *Dominicati rhetorici. Dominicatus* I take for an adjective derived from *dominicum*, "demesne," "estate." Patrick's plainly sarcastic address seems to be directed to the remnants of the highly cultured leisure class of Gaul. It would be a quite appro-

priate description of such people as Apollinaris Sidonius and his circle.

43 Cf. Heb. 12.28; 1 Thess. 2.10; etc.

44 *In mensura itaque fidei Trinitatis oportet distinguere.* In my opinion, *distinguere,* "distinguish," here as in Conf. 2 means the distinction, and accordingly the choice, between good and evil, right and wrong. There is, I think, nothing to suggest (as does F. R. M. Hitchcock, *St. Patrick and his Gallic Friends* [SPCK, London 1916] 131; *Hermathena* 47 [1932] 206) that Patrick speaks of doctrinal distinctions. If this were so, the *mensura fidei* to which he refers could be a "standard of faith," as in Rom. 2.3 (whence the expression is borrowed); but I think Patrick's belief in the Holy Trinity, his *fides Trinitatis,* is as such the standard (*mensura*) of his decision, namely, to publish his *Confession.*

45 According to seventh-century tradition, the mountain was Sliabh Mis (Slemish, Co. Antrim).

46 Patrick offered his services in lieu of payment. This can be inferred from the incidental remark, Conf. 19, that the boat carried a cargo of Irish hounds. The fact that he had been a shepherd for six years probably recommended him for their care. This would also explain why the captain who first refused the offer (did he suspect Patrick to be a fugitive slave?), so readily took him on.

47 The sucking of the breasts was a pagan rite of seeking protection. Its practice by the ancient Irish is amply attested: cf. J. Ryan, "A Difficult Phrase in the 'Confession' of St. Patrick: *reppuli sugere mammellas eorum,* §18," IER 52 (1938) 293-99; M. A. O'Brien, "Miscellanea Hibernica," *Etudes Celtiques* 3 (1938) 372 f.

48 *Per desertum.* The land may have been laid waste by the vandals early in 407, or merely abandoned either on that occasion or later in the year when the country was at the mercy of Constantine III and his soldiers (so P. Grosjean, AB 54 [1936] 196-99). See also Introd. n. 11.

49 Cf. Gen. 12.10.

50 Joel 2.12 f.

51 See above, n. 46. Doubtless these hounds were Irish wolfhounds, and their destination was probably some place in either Provence or Italy (cf. J. B. Bury, *Life of St. Patrick* [London 1905] 31, 341 f.; cf. Introd. 4). Celtic hounds are praised, es-

pecially for their swiftness, by Arrian, *Cyneg.* 1-3; cf. Strabo, *Geogr.* 4. 2.200; Jerome, *In Ier.* 3.1.3. They were in demand both for hunting and for the arena.

[52] The offering of honey was probably intended as an act of adoration, and for this reason Patrick refused it: see E. MacNeill, *St. Patrick, Apostle of Ireland* 28.

[53] 2 Peter 1.13.

[54] This strange experience testifies to a certain fusion in Patrick's mind of the prophet Elias and the sun-god Helios. This fusion was common in ancient Christian art and literature; see C & M 12.144-46. It had two causes: the similarity of their Greek name-forms (*Helias–Helios*), and the reminiscences of the sun-god in his chariot that were evoked by the fiery chariot in which the prophet was taken to heaven (4 Kings 2.11). There may have been at the back of Patrick's mind some dim recollection of a picture or mosaic representing the assumption of (H)Elias after the traditional representations of Helios driving through the sky: cf. Bieler 62; also the article, with illustrations, of H. Leclercq, "Elie, Elisée," *Dict. d'archéol. chrét. et de lit.* 4.2 (1921) 2670-74.

The sun that dispelled Patrick's nightmare was, of course, understood by him as the *sol verus* (the Messianic *Sol Iustitiae*– Mal. 4.2)–Christ. Here again we have the very interesting parallelism of a Christian tradition conceiving of Christ, the Creator of the sun, as the Sun of our salvation (*Sol Salutis*) op-posed to the pagan and Imperial sun-god (*Sol Invictus*); see esp. F. J. Dölger, *Sol Salutis* (2nd ed. Münster i.W. 1925). Christ as the true Sun and God of resurrection and salvation was also represented in art as ascending in a fiery chariot; see now the most interesting mosaic discovered in the recent excavations in St. Peter's, Rome: B. M. A. Ghetti–A. Ferrua–E. Josi–E. Kirsch-baum, *"Esplorazioni sotto la Confessione di San Pietro in Vati-cano, eseguite negli anni 1940-1949* (Vatican City 1951) 1.38-42 and pl. B, C; 2. pl. XI. The mosaic was found on the vault of a mausoleum which was originally pagan, but radically transformed into a Christian place of burial. On Christ contrasted with the pagan *Sol Invictus*, see also the Christmas sermons of Augustine in the present series: T. C. Lawler, *St. Augustine, Sermons for Christmas and Epiphany* (ACW 15, Westminster, Md.–London 1952). (For the references to *Sol Salutis* I am indebted to the Editors.)

[55] Ps. 49.15.

[56] Matt. 10.19 f.

[57] How do the "many years" of this paragraph tally with the "few years" of Conf. 23? Many solutions have been suggested, of which none is convincing: see Bieler 62. The fact that §22 resumes the narrative at the point where it has been dropped at the end of 19 marks §§20-21 as a digression. Are we perhaps justified in relegating this "second captivity" to some later period of Patrick's life, and in explaining its insertion here by a mere association of ideas?

[58] Gen. 37.21 (Sept.).

[59] The continuation of the journey described in §19.

[60] The Victoricus here mentioned cannot be identified. He seems to have been a person known to Patrick at home. Perhaps Patrick confided to him his desire to convert the Irish; this would be sufficient to explain that in his dream Patrick saw him as coming from Ireland, bringing him the message of the Irish people. The Patrick-legend made of Victoricus the angel Victor and identified the latter with the heavenly voice that announced to Patrick the end of his captivity.

[61] The identification of this locality is a crucial problem. Our sole authentic source, Patrick himself, places it near the west coast of Ireland; this gives substance to Tírechán's assertion that the wood was located near Killala, Co. Mayo. Cf. T. F. O'Rahilly, *The Two Patricks* 34 f., 60 f. At the root of the difficulties raised by modern scholars lies the unwarranted assumption that the Wood of Voclut was the place of Patrick's captivity. Once this idea is abandoned, there is no reason why the seventh-century tradition that Patrick tended the flocks of Miliuc near Sliabh Mis (see above, n. 45) should not be genuine. How Patrick came to identify the voices of his dream as coming from the Wood of Voclut is another question, the answer to which will probably never be known. See L. Bieler, "The Problem of *Silva Focluti*," *Irish Hist. Stud.* 3 (1942-43) 351-64 (with bibliography concerning the question).

[62] Dan. 3.51.

[63] 2 Cor. 12.2.

[64] 1 John 3.16.

[65] Eph. 3.16.

[66] Rom. 8.26; the relative clause at the end, *quae verbis exprimi*

non possunt, is a doublet for *inenarrabilibus* not found in the Greek or the Vulgate.

⁶⁷ 1 John 2.1, contaminated with Rom. 8.26; cf. Ps.–Augustine, *Quaestiones Veteris et Novi Testamenti*, app. 77 (p. 471.3 f. Souter): *habemus advocatum qui postulat pro peccatis nostris.*

⁶⁸ The opposition of which Patrick speaks in §§26-33 was almost certainly directed against his election to the episcopate, not, as some scholars have thought, against the conduct of his mission. This seems to follow, among other things, from Conf. 29, where Patrick says that he was rejected (*reprobatus sum*) by his "seniors," that is, his superiors in the religious community (not necessarily a monastic community) to which he belonged at that time (cf. P. Grosjean, "La 'source britannique' des Vies de S. Patrice," AB 63 [1945] 116 f.). Besides, this whole section finds its most natural interpretation in Muirchú's account (1.5-9) of the events preceding Patrick's election to the Irish episcopate. It is thus in retrospect that Patrick here calls his episcopate laborious.

⁶⁹ Cf. Deut. 24.15; 1 Par. 21.3; 2 Tim. 4.16.

⁷⁰ Cf. 2 Cor. 12.2 f.

⁷¹ Cf. Dan. 7.13.

⁷² This passage is difficult to interpret. I think that Patrick saw his own face, with a legend, as on a coin or medallion, literally "against it"; but the legend gave his bare name, without the title "bishop."

⁷³ The reading of the non-Irish MSS *dei signati* (*designati* Book of Armagh) has been defended by J. MacErleann (cf. D. S. Nerney, "A Study of St. Patrick's Sources," I, IER 71 [1949] 504 n. 1), who saw in it a person's name, Deisignatus, the Latin equivalent of Greek *Theosphragistos*. This would then be the person that revealed Patrick's sin (Conf. 27) before the British synod (Conf. 32). If this be accepted, the traditional view that Patrick deliberately suppressed the name of his former friend (*designati nudato nomine* "of a person called openly by his name") would have to be abandoned. On the contrary, Patrick would have felt compelled by divine authority to reveal that name which otherwise he would have kept secret "for the love of Christ" (Conf. 33). The name Deisignatus seems unique; the bishop of Maastricht whom Nerney mentions as a possible namesake (died *c.* 520) is spelled *Designatus* in Latin documents.

⁷⁴ Zach. 2.8.

[75] 1 Tim. 1.12.

[76] John 10.29. For an interpretation of this paragraph, see the Introd. 5. Patrick's description of the synod in question as a "defence" probably means that the several candidates had to be defended by their sponsors against any objection that might be made to their persons.

[77] 2 Par. 6.37; and often.

[78] Rom. 8.11.

[79] Ps. 94.9.

[80] *Ibid.* 33.7. In the following there are reminiscences of 2 Kings 7.18 and Ps. 45.11 and 33.4.

[81] The words "in the last days" (cf. Acts 2.17) need not imply chiliastic views. There is no evidence to show that St. Patrick thought the end of the world imminent. According to his geographical knowledge, Ireland was the sole country outside the Roman Empire, which he identified with Christendom. With his mission, the command of Christ, "Go ye and teach all nations," seemed fulfilled, and thus the "last days" seemed to have come. But Patrick does not speculate about their duration. He certainly looked forward to a long period of Christian life in Ireland (cf. *propter spem perennitatis*, Conf. 49). The same theme as here is favoured elsewhere in his writings—cf. Conf. 40 and Epist. 11. One wonders how he reconciled with it his knowledge of the presence of heathens, namely the various Teutonic tribes, on Roman territory (cf. his remark about the Franks, Epist. 14). Is it that he adopted the strictly legal view according to which they were Roman subjects—whose conversion was purely a matter of time?

[82] Cf. Matt. 24.14.

[83] These "twelve dangers" cannot be identified with particular incidents in Patrick's life; perhaps this is simply an allusion to 2 Cor. 11.26 (so Nerney, "A Study of St. Patrick's Sources," IV, IER 72 [1949] 269).

[84] Matt. 13.54.

[85] Cf. Ps. 35.8.

[86] The words "in sorrow and tears" seem to indicate that these gifts were offered by penitents. Patrick refused to accept them in order to avoid even the appearance of "selling" absolution.—As a bishop in Ireland, Patrick had of course no "superiors" (*seniores*). Whether any of his former superiors went with him as advisers we do not know. It is just as likely that Patrick is

speaking here of some fellow missionaries who, being his elders, objected to his action on the grounds of their greater experience.

[87] Ecclus. 29.30.

[88] Here and Conf. 51 the word for administering the sacrament of confirmation is *consummare* (corresponding to Greek τελειοῦν). Cf. Cyprian, *Epist.* 73.9; Hilary, *In Matt.* 2.4.

[89] Jer. 16.19 (Sept.), followed by Acts 13.47 (Isa. 49.6).

[90] Matt. 8.11.

[91] Matt. 4.19; Mark 1.17.

[92] Cf. Jer. 16.16.—"And so on": the plural "through the prophets" indicates that a second prophecy followed (as above at the end of §38)—perhaps Ezech. 47.10. Patrick certainly quoted both texts in full. The mere indication of familiar Biblical passages by giving their initial words only is an all too common device of Irish scribes; in the present instance it goes back to the ancestor of all our MSS; cf. C & M 12.169 f.

[93] Matt. 28.19 f.

[94] Mark 16.15 f.

[95] Matt. 24.14.

[96] Joel 2.28 f. as quoted in Acts 2.17 f.

[97] Osee 1.10 as quoted in Rom. 9.25 f.

[98] *Nuntius Dei.* Even *nuntius* alone is occasionally used for "angel," cf. Gildas, *De excidio Britanniae* 1.p.27.13 f. Mommsen. According to C. Mohrmann, *Die altchristliche Sondersprache in den Sermones des hl. Augustin* (Latinitas Christianorum primaeva 3, Nijmegen 1932) 79, *nuntius* was intended as an interpretation of Greek ἄγγελος rather than as a permanent translation (so, e.g., in the sermons of St. Augustine).

[99] In St. Patrick's time this attitude was perfectly legitimate. Later, when Ireland had become Christian, the consent of the parents was required ("Second Synod of St. Patrick," canon 27: Haddan and Stubbs 2.2.333 ff. For this as for other reasons the attribution of this canon to St. Patrick is impossible; the whole set of canons was probably enacted by some Irish synod of the seventh century—see Bury, *Life of St. Patrick* 339). As regards the sixth century, there is the story of St. Columbanus (Jonas of Bobbio, *Life of St. Columbanus* 1.3), who stepped over the body of his mother when she threw herself at his feet imploring him to renounce his monastic vocation.

[100] Married people who renounced the exercise of their marital rights were a recognised class of the faithful in the early Church;

cf., for example, Novatian, *De bono pudicitiae* 4. Regarding the class or order of widows (*viduatus*), see the observations in ACW 13.121 n. 66, and 15.215 n. 6.

[101] In Christian antiquity the adjectives *sanctus* and *beatus* commonly refer to the just on earth; so Greek ἅγιοι, "the holy," already in the New Testament (Acts 26.10; etc.). Cf. C & M 12.174.

[102] 2 Peter 1.13.

[103] 2 Tim. 1.9.

[104] Here and in the following there are reminiscences of John 14.26 and Exod. 20.6 (Apoc. 5.11?).

[105] *Conservi*—used to designate "fellow Christians" since Tertullian; cf. S. W. J. Teeuwen, *Sprachlicher Bedeutungswandel bei Tertullian* (Studien zur Geschichte und Kultur des Altertums 14.1, Paderborn 1926) 127 f.

[106] Prov. 10.1; 15.20; cf. 17.6.

[107] A conflation of Matt. 18.7 and Rom. 2.24.

[108] 2 Cor. 11.6.

[109] The *virgines sanctae*, together with the virgins of the other sex—*confessores*, were an important group among the faithful of a local church. The liturgy provided for a solemn reception (*consecratio, benedictio virginum*) of the former on certain high feast days—cf. the sermon delivered by Pope Liberius at the reception of Marcellina, the sister of St. Ambrose (Ambrose, *De virginibus* 1.3). See also T. C. Lawler's remarks on St. Augustine's *Serm.* 192: ACW 15.214 n.10.

[110] The *screpall* was a small silver coin, see H. d'Arbois de Jubainville, *Revue Celtique* 18 (1897) 114; N. J. D. White, *Libri Sancti Patricii* 295.

[111] 1 Kings 12.3.

[112] *Ibid.*

[113] Patrick obviously means to say that he had often to bribe local rulers in order to get their permission to preach the Gospel in their respective territories.

[114] That is, "for my protection."

[115] Ancient Ireland was divided into a great number of small states (*tuatha*) which often were at war with one another. Thus the protection of the Irish princes who escorted Patrick on his missionary journeys might at times be of doubtful value. Patrick, however, had made friends of the other party as well, who, though somewhat belatedly, came to his rescue. This is my ten-

tative reconstruction of the incident to which Patrick refers—cf. "St. Patrick and the Irish People," *Rev. of Politics* 10 (1948) 298.

[116] The kings, not the *brehons* (lawyers) who were merely expert advisers; cf. E. MacNeill, *Early Irish Laws and Institutions* (Dublin 1935) 99. The local rulers had it in their power either to admit Patrick or to bar him from their lands; their goodwill had often to be bought with money (see above, n. 113).

[117] 2 Cor. 12.15.

[118] Conflation of 2 Cor. 1.23 and Gal. 1.20.

[119] Conflation of Heb. 10.23 and Titus 1.2. *Numquam* (for *non*) *mentitur* has no authority in any Biblical text; it is Patrick's own intensification.

[120] Acts 20.24.

[121] Ps. 54.23.

[122] 1 Peter 4.19.

[123] Eph. 6.20.

[124] Deut. 10.17; Gal. 2.6.

[125] Ps. 115.12.

[126] *Ibid.* 7.10; Apoc. 2.23.

[127] This and the following paragraph are translated and exploited by F. J. Dölger—"Das Sonnengleichnis in einer Weihnachtspredigt des Bischofs Zeno von Verona: Christus als wahre und ewige Sonne," *Antike u. Christentum* 6 (1940) 22 f.—in a collection of early Christian texts exemplifying the concept of Christ as the true and eternal Sun (as opposed to the deified sun —*Sol Invictus*—of the Roman Empire; cf. above, n. 54).

[128] Rom. 8.17.

[129] *Ibid.* 8.29.

[130] *Ibid.* 11.36.

[131] 1 John 2.17, with interpolation of a clause from John 12.34, as in Cyprian, Augustine, and other Western Fathers.

[132] 2 Tim. 4.1; 1 Tim. 5.21; cf. Matt. 16.27; Mark 8.38.

[133] See Introd. 8, with n. 31.

LETTER TO THE SOLDIERS OF COROTICUS

[1] This title, though not quite adequate (cf. P. Grosjean, AB 63 [1945] 100 ff.), is suggested by §2.

[2] Phil. 2.30.

[3] "Holy" are the Romans (that is, the citizens of the Roman

Empire) in so far as they are Christians. The soldiers of Coroticus, nominal Christians though they were, had through their
hostile action forfeited the title of Romans, because for Patrick
"Romans" and "Christians" are identical terms. Coroticus and
his subjects were (technically) Roman citizens quite as well as
was Patrick; but—so Patrick maintains—they live after the fashion
of the enemies of Rome (spiritual Rome as well as secular Rome)
and even associate with them: *ritu hostili in morte vivunt, socii
Scottorum atque Pictorum.*

[4] *Apostata* can denote either the apostate or the heretic. We
do not know in what sense or on what grounds Patrick here and
Epist. 15 applies the term to the Picts; it might even be applied
loosely (= "sinners"), as in the case of the murmuring Jews,
Num. 14.9 (Greek and Old Latin)—cf. C. Mohrmann, *op. cit.*
81 f.

[5] These words, in my opinion, are nothing more than a cir-
cumlocution for "whom I have baptised." See my commentary,
C & M 12.195.

[6] *Zabulus.* This spelling of the word *diabolus*, common in late
Latin, is characteristic of the "Irish" group of Vulgate texts; cf.
C & M 12.196.

[7] John 8.34 (the omission of *peccati* after *servus* is an early
"western" variant); cf. 44.

[8] Eph. 6.20; cf. Conf. 56.

[9] A conflation of Acts 20.29 and Ps. 52.5 (cf. 13.4).

[10] Ps. 118.126.

[11] Rom. 8.30 and Acts 13.47.

[12] Patrick's words echo clearly St. Cyprian, *Epist.* 59.2: . . .
de ecclesiae gubernandae sublimi et divina potestate.

[13] Matt. 16.19; 18.18.

[14] Dan. 3.87.

[15] The implication is that these people are to be excommunicated. To dine with sinners was forbidden on the authority of
St. Paul, 1 Cor. 5.11; that not even the alms of an excommunicated person should be accepted was provided in canon 12 of the
synod of Patrick, Auxilius, and Iserninus (see above, 51).

[16] The original has *crudeliter*—an apt description of penitential
discipline in ancient Ireland (cf. C & M 12.198).

[17] Ecclus. 34.23 f. (*reprobat* for *non probat* is a typically Hi-
bernian variant).

[18] Job 20.15 f., 26. Patrick's text is very close to that of Codex

Alexandrinus. It would appear that Patrick read these three verses in immediate succession. He would then have had before him one of those defective copies of the Book of Job about which St. Jerome so poignantly complains. See L. Bieler, "Der Bibeltext des heiligen Patrick," *Biblica* 28 (1947) 35-37.

[19] Hab. 2.6.

[20] Matt. 16.26.

[21] The term "mortal sin," *peccatum mortale,* seems to have been coined by St. Cyprian (cf. *De bono patient.* 14), obviously after 1 John 5.16 f.

[22] Rom. 13.9 (Exod. 20.13, 17).

[23] 1 John 3.15; cf. Cyprian, *De dom. orat.* 24.

[24] 1 John 3.14.

[25] Cf. Acts 13.47.

[26] *Decurio* is a member of the city council in a Roman municipality. There were also *decuriones militum,* military officers of minor rank. The possibility that Patrick's father belonged to the latter class was contemplated by P. Grosjean (cf. n. 1 to the Introd.). From all that Patrick tells us about his home life, however, it seems far more likely that he grew up in one of the cities of the south-west than in a garrison town of the military zone between the walls.

[27] Cf. Rom. 6.23.

[28] John 4.44.

[29] *Ibid.* 10.16.

[30] Eph. 4.6 (or Mal. 2.10? Matt. 23.9?); cf. below, §16.

[31] Matt. 12.30; cf. Luke 11.23.

[32] Ecclus. 34.28; cf. Gal. 2.18.

[33] 1 Cor. 13.5; cf. 2 Cor. 12.14.

[34] 2 Cor. 8.16.

[35] This is an allusion to Jer. 16.16 and Acts 2.17—both quoted in Conf. 40. On the idea, see above n. 81 to the Confessio.

[36] Matt. 7.15.

[37] Ecclus. 9.17, loosely quoted.

[38] The Franks were still heathens in St. Patrick's time; they did not accept the Christian faith until 496. Even in Merovingian Gaul the ransoming of captives was one of the chief charities; see J. N. Garvin, *The Vitas Sanctorum Patrum Emeretensium* (The Cath. Univ. of America studies in Mediaeval and Renaissance Latin Language and Literature 19, Washington 1946) 420 f.

[39] Rom. 1.32.

[40] *Ibid.* 12.15.

[41] 1 Cor. 12.26. The un-Biblical subjunctive (*"let* all members grieve with it"*) has a parallel in Tertullian, *De paen.* 10.5: *condoleat universum (corpus cum uno membro).*

[42] Cf. above, §14. The captives had been sold partly to the Picts, partly to the sections of Ireland which had not yet become Christian—an indication that the Letter falls on a comparatively early date in St. Patrick's life as a missionary. The present passage, however, gives the impression that Patrick thinks in the first place of the Picts. They are, therefore, to be understood primarily under the "foreign nation that has no knowledge of God" (§14). Whether the description, here and in §2, of the Picts as apostates implies heresy or relapse into paganism, we do not know; in either event Patrick could say that they did not know God.

[43] The address or apostrophe of the victims, technically a rhetorical fiction, comes natural enough here as an outlet for the writer's emotion.

[44] Ps. 64.4, contaminated with Ezech. 18.20; 33.12.

[45] Cf. Ps. 68.9. For Patrick, Romans and Christians are identical—see above n. 3. Hence in his opinion the Irish, once baptised, were, technically speaking, "Romans" (cf. *Sayings of Patrick* 3). On the other hand, he counts himself as one of them, and shares the contempt in which they are held. Coroticus, however, adopts a different view. For him Patrick and his flock are "aliens."

[46] Mal. 2.10.

[47] Apoc. 22.5 and 21.4.

[48] Mal. 4.2 f. Patrick's text is identical with that of St. Augustine, *City of God* 18.35.

[49] *Cum apostolis et prophetis atque martyribus.* The unchronological sequence *apostolis—prophetis—martyribus* recalls a passage in St. Cyprian (*De mort.* 26) and a more familiar passage in the *Te Deum:*

> Te gloriosus *apostolorum* chorus,
> Te *prophetarum* laudabilis numerus,
> Te *martyrum* candidatus laudat exercitus.

The theory proposed by responsible scholars (Morin, Burn) that Nicetas of Remesiana (*c.* 335–414) is the author, or rather, the composer (or compositor), of the hymn, rests principally upon the tradition of a number of Irish manuscripts. In the present passage we may well have the earliest evidence of the *Te Deum* in Ireland. Cf. C & M 12.207.

[50] Matt. 8.11; cf. Conf. 39.

[51] Apoc. 22.15.

[52] *Ibid*. 21.8.

[53] 1 Peter 4.18, with the words "transgressor of the law" inserted, probably from James 2.11.

[54] This "quotation" is made up of several bits of Biblical phrases: Wisd. 5.15, Ps. 67.3 f., Wisd. 5.1 and 3.8. The conflation has resulted in the particularly strange combination, *iusti epulentur in magna constantia*.

[55] 2 Tim. 4.1 and 1 Tim. 5.21.

[56] Mark 16.15 f.; cf. Conf. 40.

[57] The Biblical phrase (Ps. 59.8; 107.8) is used here for marking the preceding text as a quotation.

[58] Instead of the usual *Pax vobiscum*, which would here be out of place, Patrick concludes with a wish that peace may be restored with the Holy Trinity, in other words, that the guilty should make their peace with God. Cf. C & M 12.210.

FRAGMENTS

[1] A similar experience is described in Conf. 24, but this fragment cannot belong there (though the possibility of a lacuna in the text cannot be denied) because of the words, "whether within me, or beside me, I know not," which cannot be reconciled with the statement of the present passage to the effect that Patrick heard the voices *within* him.

[2] The episode told here of Patrick's life—the sole known instance of his exercise of metropolitan jurisdiction—is preserved in two slightly different versions: in the *Book of Armagh*, fol. 9r, a, and in a British Museum MS (Cotton Otho E.XIII). P. Grosjean, who has made a detailed study of these traditions—"Notes sur les documents anciens concernant S. Patrice," AB 62 (1944) 44-46, 51-60—comes to the following conclusions: 1. The account of this episode is probably derived from the files of Tírechán which were to be used for a continuation of his *Breviarium de sancto Patricio*. 2. The quotation of Patrick's words seems to be taken from the letter, or letters, which he wrote on that occa-

sion. 3. The discrepancy of the names in our sources (Caetiacus and Sacellus—Cechianus and Conall) can be explained on the assumption that Conall, the young king of the territory, was mistaken for a bishop by the redactor of the note in the Cottonian MS. Conall, himself a disciple of Céthech (Caetiacus, Cechianus), would, in his capacity as local ruler, share with the two bishops the responsibility for their arbitrary procedure; hence Patrick had good reason for writing to him as well as to them. —According to T. F. O'Rahilly, *The Two Patricks* 28 f., Cethiacus and Sacellus were disciples of the "earlier Patricius" (i.e. Palladius, as O'Rahilly maintains on the doubtful authority of a note in the *Book of Armagh*, 16r, a; see L. Bieler, "Was Palladius surnamed Patricius?", *Studies* 32 [1943] 323-26; "The Mission of Palladius," *Traditio* 6 [1948] 8), whom the later Patricius, the author of our texts, forced into submission.

³ A plain in the northern part of Co. Roscommon.

⁴ *Pueri Patricii.* "In the life of St. Patrick there are various references to the *pueri Patricii*, the boys who accompanied him, being trained for the clerical state which they wished to embrace": J. Ryan, "The Two Patricks," IER 60 (1942) 251. Caetiacus and Sacellus probably began their ecclesiastical career in this way.

⁵ *In libris Patrici.* They were probably books *about* St. Patrick, but they cannot be identified more accurately. See C & M 11. 25 n. 47.

⁶ As many other disciples of St. Patrick, the bishops in question had apparently taken monastic vows prior to their appointment; cf. the expression *fecerunt poenitentiam monachorum* in the parallel text in the *Book of Armagh*.

SAYINGS OF PATRICK

¹ These "sayings" of Patrick are prefixed to the work of Tírechán in the *Book of Armagh*, fol. 9r, a.

² This *dictum* was known to Tírechán (*Book of Armagh*, fol. 9r, b), who remarks that Patrick said so *in commemoratione laborum*. A written source is probable, but *Commemoratio laborum* was hardly its title. Tírechán's master, bishop Ultan, gave the additional information that Patrick stayed for thirty years in one of these islands, namely the *insola Aralanensis*, which has often been identified with Lérins. There is, however, no

genuine evidence to the effect that Patrick stayed at Lérins. Patrick's Bible text differs from all known Lérins writers (cf. L. Bieler, *Biblica* 28 [1947] 258 f.); there are also chronological difficulties—cf. J. Ussher, *Britannicarum ecclesiarum antiquitates* (Dublin 1639) 836; P. Grosjean, "Notes chronologiques sur le séjour de S. Patrice en Gaule," AB 63 (1945) 91 f. I am therefore inclined—with R. Louis, "Le séjour de Saint Patrice à Auxerre," *Mélanges . . . Louis Halphen* (Paris 1951) 445-51—to regard *insola Aralanensis* as the name of a place at or near Auxerre, where Patrick was trained under St. Germanus.

³ This pious phrase (*Deo gratias*) may very well have been a favourite saying of Patrick. It occurs repeatedly in his writings (Conf. 19, 23, 42; Epist. 17).

⁴ This dictum is problematical. Modern literature on the question has been listed by Bieler 129 n. 14. With P. Grosjean (in his review of B. Capelle, "Le Kyrie de la messe et le pape Gélase," *Rev. Bénéd.* 46 [1934] 126-44), AB 52 (1934) 410 f., I think it likely that the first part, "Church of the Irish, nay of the Romans," is a separate saying, and a genuine one of Patrick's. As regards the continuation, which P. Grosjean considers spurious, it is more difficult to decide. I am inclined to believe that it is based on a genuine *dictum* which recommended the singing of *Deo gratias* at all canonical hours, and that the introduction of the *Kyrie eleison* is interpolated. I note, however, that the language of the whole differs considerably from that of the genuine writings of St. Patrick.—A different interpretation has been attempted by C. A. Bolton, "St. Patrick's Pastoral Testament," IER 74 (1950) 234-41. The only point on which I can agree with the writer is his interpretation of *omni hora orationis* as "at all canonical hours."

CANONS

¹ See Introd. 13. Auxilius and Iserninus, together with Secundinus, joined Patrick as auxiliary bishops in 439.—For the text, cf. J. Hardouin, *Conciliorum collectio* 1 (Paris 1715) 1790-93; J. D. Mansi, *Sacrorum conciliorum nova et amplissima collectio* 6 (Florence 1761) 515-19. I have followed the text offered by Haddan-Stubbs, *Councils and Ecclesiastical Documents relating to Great Britain and Ireland* 2.2 (Oxford 1878) 327-29, which, except for linguistic minutiae, is a faithful copy of the sole in-

dependent MS of this text, Cambridge, Corpus Christi College 279, saec. IX/X. See also C. J. Hefele–H. Leclercq, *Histoire des conciles* 2.2 (Paris 1908) 888-95.

[2] Ecclus. 20.2.

[3] Decrees against vagrant clerics were issued by various councils from that of Nicaea onwards; see the materials collected by H. Waddell, *The Wandering Scholars* (London 1927) 244 ff., where the Irish canon is overlooked.

[4] This canon and the next either refer to indigent clerics (cf. Leclercq, *op. cit.* 889 f.) or belong together with canon 1.

[5] The Roman custom consisted in the shaving of the entire crown, and was thus distinct from the native (druidic) tonsure which extended only from one ear to the other. This canon was defended by Bury, *Life of St. Patrick* 239-43, against the assertion made in the eighth-century *Catalogus sanctorum Hiberniae* (Haddan-Stubbs 2.2.292) that in St. Patrick's time there was only one tonsure, *de aure ad aurem*.

[6] The text does not make it clear whether this clause applies only to clerics in minor orders, or reckons also with the possibility that a married man might become a deacon or priest.–In a story preserved in the *Book of Armagh* (fol. 18r, probably part of Tírechán's files), St. Patrick, wishing to appoint a bishop for Leinster, asks Dubthach for a suitable candidate; he should, among other things, be "a man of one wife only" (*fer oínsétche*). This is, of course, a deliberate reminiscence of 1 Tim. 3.2; Titus, 1.6. But it shows at least that a seventh-century hagiographer thought it possible for a bishop in St. Patrick's time to have a wife. J. Ryan, *Irish Monasticism* (Dublin 1931) 86 and n. 1, explains Patrick's choice of Dubthach's disciple Fiacc as dictated by the great difficulty of finding an unmarried native candidate qualified for the position, and remarks that according to the ecclesiastical legislation of the time, Fiacc, once elected bishop, would have been obliged either to renounce his wife or live with her as a sister.

[7] *Alienus*, that is, excommunicated.

[8] This implies that he had been tonsured. Such a psalmist (*psalmista*) or chanter (*cantor*) who led the faithful in singing the psalms, apparently is not to be confused with the minor cleric known as *lector*; cf. H. Leclercq, "Psalmista," *Dict. d'archéol. chrét. et de lit.* 14.2 (1948) 1944.

[9] The druids, a body of native scholars, were the guardians of

the pagan traditions of Ireland. Being referred to here as *haruspices*, they apparently also practiced magic. In the Patrick legend, where they are depicted as the sworn enemies of Patrick's mission, they are both teachers of paganism and sorcerers.—The act of taking an oath before a pagan druid constituted idolatry. This and the other two sins mentioned, murder and adultery, from ancient Christianity formed the triad of capital sins (*principalia delicta, peccata capitalia, irremissibilia,* etc.); cf. B. Poschmann, *Paenitentia secunda* (Theophaneia 1, Bonn 1940) 321-25.

[10] The MS (see n. 1) reads *renuetur*, which is probably meant to represent *renovetur*.

[11] *Lamia*. This was originally an individual monster; but popular superstition among the Greeks and especially among the Romans conceived of a large number of *lamiae*, who were thought to be vampire-like demons. Cf. W. H. Roscher, *Ausführliches Lexikon der griechischen und römischen Mythologie* 2.2 (1894-97) 1819 f.; C. Daremberg—E. Saglio, *Dictionnaire des antiquités grecques et romaines* 3 (1904) 908 f.; Pauly-Wissowa-Kroll, *Realencyclopädie der classischen Altertumswissenschaft* 12.1 (1924) 544 f. Hence *lamia* came to be used as a common noun meaning "witch."

[12] I read *deliquerit* for *dereliquerit* of the MS.

[13] Just as a Christian is not allowed to swear before a druid he is also forbidden to sue a person in a pagan court of law. It seems difficult to reconcile with this canon the story about the revision of the traditional Irish law (the *Senchas Mór*) in a Christian spirit, with the active collaboration of St. Patrick; cf. *Ancient Laws of Ireland* 1 (London 1865) 1-8.

[14] The paying of a bride-price was an Indo-European practice. For ancient Ireland, see O. Schrader, *Reallexikon der indogermanischen Altertumskunde* (Strasbourg 1901) 110; J. A. MacCulloch, *The Mythology of All Races* (Boston 1918) 130: "Celtic Mythology."

[15] This canon safeguards episcopal jurisdiction against possible encroachment on the part of lay authority. Cf. above, 48, Fragment 2 and n. 2 to same.

[16] This provision certainly has its root in the custom of administering solemn baptism during Easter Night, at the end of the forty days' fast. The sole early Irish baptismal rite that we know (*Stowe Missal, c.* 800 A.D., fol. 47r-58v) is not connected

with the Paschal ceremonies as is, for instance, that in the Gelasian Sacramentary.

[17] *Paruchia*, that is "diocese"; cf. W. Stokes, *The Tripartite Life of Patrick* 2 (1887) 665.

[18] This was probably a safeguard against the infiltration of Semi-Pelagianism—see Introd. 5. On this assumption, the canon could well be genuine (cf. n. 43 to the Introd.).

[19] With the words, *nec cibum ministrare decet*, we have, I think, to understand a complement in the dative (*ei*), not a subject accusative (*eum*). A deacon—here a monk, it would seem —deserting his abbot, and failing the presbyter or priest whom he is sent to assist, would forfeit his title to sustenance. Cf. Bury, *Life of St. Patrick* 244.

ST. SECUNDINUS
HYMN ON ST. PATRICK

INTRODUCTION

[1] Cf. F. J. A. Raby, *A History of Christian Latin Poetry* (Cambridge 1927) 134 f.

[2] See the calendar under November 27 in *The Martyrology of Oengus the Culdee* (*c.* 800), ed. by W. Stokes (Henry Bradshaw Society 29, London 1905) 237. The entries in the *Notulae* of the *Book of Armagh*, fol. 19 r, a—*reliquiae ymnus Berach Brig doas*—almost certainly refer to a series of incidents connected with Secundinus as told in the *Tripartite Life of Patrick*. The *Book of Armagh* was written about 807 A. D. If the *Notulae*, as P. Grosjean, "Que sont les Notulae?" AB 62 (1944) 66-70, suggests, were part of an index to Tírechán's files, the attribution of the hymn to Secundinus would be attested even for the seventh century. See G. F. Hamilton, *In St. Patrick's Praise* (2nd ed. Dublin 1920) 10 f.

[3] Annals of Ulster, ed. W. M. Hennessy, vol. 1, and Annals of Innisfallen, ed. S. Mac Airt, under the years 439 and 447; see Bieler 90.

[4] Preface to *Audite omnes* in the Franciscan MS of the Irish *Liber Hymnorum*; similarly, *Leabhar Breac* (Dublin, Royal Irish Academy, MS 23.P.16, written before 1411).

[5] Cf. E. MacNeill, "The Hymn of St. Secundinus in Honour of St. Patrick," *Irish Hist. Stud.* 2 (1939-40) 129.

[6] See above, n. 4.

[7] Above, n. 4.

[8] "Notes d'hagiographie celtique, 10," AB 63 (1945) 111.

[9] On all this, see Hamilton, *op. cit.* 5-15; MacNeill, *art. cit.* 129-53.

[10] Ed. M. Petschenig, *Corpus scriptorum ecclesiasticorum latinorum* 51 (1908) 3 ff. Cf. Raby, *op. cit.* 20 ff.

[11] This is the third item in an enumeration of the four "special honours" of St. Patrick in Ireland—an interesting document concerning devotion to St. Patrick in the seventh century.

[12] Line 51 (*Thesaurus Palaeohibernicus* 2 [Cambridge 1903]

319). This is the glossator's interpretation in the Franciscan MS of the *Liber Hymnorum*. Bernard and Atkinson, 2. 176, consider the possibility that the poet meant the *Lorica*, on which see below, the Appendix.

[13] This seems to have been a common practice if a hymn was long. The hymn, *Christus in nostra insula* (Bernard and Atkinson 1. 14 f.; C. Blume, *Analecta Hymnica* 51. 317 f.), for example, is probably a remnant of the last three stanzas of another abecedarian hymn (Bernard and Atkinson 1. xxi f.; Blume, *ibid*. 345). In the case of Secundinus hymn this privilege is said to have been obtained from St. Patrick himself—cf. the Preface in the Franciscan MS: "When Sechnall had finished making this eulogy, he went to show it to Patrick, to whom he said: 'I have made a eulogy for a certain son of life and I should like thee to hear it.' 'My welcome to a eulogy of the household of God,' said Patrick. But Sechnall began his hymn at *Beata Christi* (i.e. the second stanza), that Patrick should not hear for whom it was made till the whole should have been recited. However, when Sechnall uttered *Maximus in regno caelorum*, Patrick said, 'How could a man be *maximus in caelo?*' Secundinus said, 'The superlative here stands for the positive.' On the conclusion of the recital Sechnall said, '(Give) me the reward of it.' 'Thou shalt have it,' said Patrick, 'the number of hairs that are on thy cloak, i.e., on the hood, the like number of sinners (shall go) to heaven for the hymn.' 'I will not take that,' said Sechnall. 'Thou shalt have,' said Patrick, 'this boon: every one who shall recite it at lying down and rising up shall go to heaven.' 'I accept that,' said Sechnall, 'but the hymn is long, and not every one will be able to commit it to memory.' 'Its grace,' said Patrick, 'shall be on the last three *capitula* (i.e. stanzas).' '*Deo gratias*,' said Sechnall." (The translation from the Irish is by Bernard and Atkinson.)

TEXT

[1] This is the title of our hymn in the Antiphonary of Bangor.

[2] Cf. Matt. 16. 18. Patrick is the head of the Irish Church as Peter is the head of the Universal Church. The parallel between the see of Patrick and the see of Peter (Armagh-Rome) is often elaborated by Irish writers.—That Patrick obtained his apostolate from God, is an echo of the saint's own words, Epist. 1.

[3] The term "barbarian" would apply to all people outside the Roman Empire. In this sense the Irish were "barbarians" (i.e.

foreigners) even for Patrick (cf. Epist. 1). The term might be used here as representing Patrick's point of view, but its choice would be more significant if Secundinus actually came from the continent of Europe.

[4] Cf. Matt. 25. 14 ff.

[5] Cf. Heb. 10. 24.

[6] Cf. Gal. 4. 14. This is certainly an exaggeration. The writings of St. Patrick abound in references to attacks of his person as well as of his vocation. The overstatement is understandable as a reply to Patrick's critics.

[7] *Christi portat stigmata,* cf. Gal. 6. 17 (Old Latin). The sufferings which Patrick had to endure in the course of his mission (cf. Conf. 35 ff.) may have left their marks in his body; perhaps Patrick himself referred to them as "marks of Christ." Cf. Hamilton, *op. cit.* 39.

[8] Cf. Gal. 6. 14.

[9] The whole stanza, with its Biblical imagery (cf. Matt. 15. 32 ff.), refers to Patrick's preaching. Cf. v. 59.

[10] Cf. Rom. 12. 1 (and 1 Thess. 4.4?). In Conf. 34 Patrick applies these words of St. Paul to himself.

[11] Cf. Matt. 5. 14 f.

[12] This is possibly an allusion to the eucharistic Mass.

[13] This stanza conveys the impression that the hymn was written in circumstances such as would have prompted St. Patrick's *Confession;* see Introd. 12, with n. 39. Patrick's spirit in adversity is illustrated briefly in Conf. 55.

[14] Cf. John 10. 11, and Patrick's words in Conf. 53.

[15] The idea of *militia caelestis* is a commonplace in the writings of St. Cyprian; cf. *De lapsis* 2; *Epist.* 10. 4; 64. 8; etc.

[16] E. MacNeill explains the "heavenly rations" (*caelestis annona*) as the material equipment of Patrick's clergy, which, apart from the liturgical vestments, would consist mainly of books (*divinis . . . sacrisque affatibus,* "books of Scripture and books of ritual"): "The Hymn of St. Secundinus . . .," *Irish Hist. Stud.* 2 (1939-40) 149 ff. The stanza would thus imply the copying of books.

[17] Cf. Matt. 22. 11 f.

[18] In the West communion under both species was the rule down to the twelfth century; cf. L. Eisenhofer, *Grundriss der Liturgik des römischen Ritus* (5th ed. by J. Lechner, Freiburg i. Br. 1950) 257 f. The words of our hymn, however, need not

necessarily contain a reference to the rite of Holy Communion. They may be meant allegorically as well as literally.

[19] The name *Israel* was often interpreted as *videns Deum*, "seeing God": cf. Eusebius, *Praep. Evang.* 11.6; Jerome, *In Isa.* 1. 1; Augustine, *Enarr. in Ps.* 75.2; 97.3; etc.

[20] The hymns which Patrick used to sing are probably not only the Canticles of Holy Scripture but also compositions of more recent times; there is some evidence to show that Patrick knew the *Te Deum laudamus* (e.g. Epist. 18 *cum apostolis et prophetis atque martyribus*). Cf. L. Bieler, *Biblica* 28 (1947) 239; cf. above, n. 49 to the Epist.

[21] *Quam legem in Trinitate sacri credit nominis.* That in his preaching Patrick should place great emphasis on the dogma of the Holy Trinity is what one would expect in his time; in fact, he uses a phrase very similar to the last line of the present stanza at the end of his "Creed" (Conf. 4). But what "this law" means in the present context remains obscure, except that Patrick would naturally explain the sacred texts in the light of his belief in the Trinitarian God—*in mensura fidei Trinitatis* (Conf. 14). An alternative explanation has been suggested to me by Dr. Plumpe: "Holding to this principle of *three* (in his song), Patrick also applies the same in his belief in the Trinity. Yet (v. 88) he teaches that this threefold (triune) God is only one substance or nature."

[22] As the Apostles were promised by Christ that they would "sit on twelve seats judging the twelve tribes of Israel" (Matt. 19. 28; Luke 22. 30), so Patrick, the "Apostle of the Irish," will judge "his" tribe at the Last Judgment. In the *Life* by Muirchú (2. 6) Patrick is formally granted this privilege and is so advised by an angel shortly before his death. Muirchú almost certainly develops the theme of Secundinus' hymn.

APPENDIX

THE *LORICA*

INTRODUCTION

[1] "A linguist would tend to regard it as an eighth-century hymn; the written exemplar to which our copies go back was written down in the ninth century"; so Prof. G. Murphy in a private communication (see end of Introd.).

[2] Prof. M. A. O'Brien (see end of Introd.) writes to me: "I have always thought the *Lorica* was very old for the following reasons: a) the syntax shows features common to the earliest (6th cent.?) archaic poems; b) it seems to be in a broken-down form of metre (⅞ syllable lines with heptasyllabic endings) which is characteristic of the earliest legal documents; and c) the sentiments expressed are such as one would scarcely find later on. It may not go back to Patrick, but I am certain it was originally composed at a very early time and then handed down orally."

[3] *Dictionary of the Irish Language* 3 (Dublin 1950) 101, 84-102, 15.

[4] See Kenney, index *s.v.* "Loricae." On the *Lorica* of St. Patrick, see *ibid.* 272-74.

TEXT

[1] Loegaire (Laogaire), according to the Irish Annals, was "high king" (*árd-rí*), that is, sovereign king of all Ireland, from 428 to 462. He was a son of Niall "of the Nine Hostages." The impressive story of St. Patrick's preaching before Loegaire at the first Easter following his landing in Ireland is told (after an earlier source, now lost) by Tírechán and Muirchú, and, on the authority of the latter, in all the later *Lives* of St. Patrick.

[2] Tara, in Co. Meath, was the residence of the "high kings" of Ireland.

[3] Benén (St. Benignus) was one of the earliest disciples of St. Patrick and succeeded him in the see of Armagh. When he first

joined Patrick, he was still a boy, and so he is said to have appeared to the assassins as a fawn.

[4] Smiths were supposed to have magic power. The smith's curse, practised by the rite of "turning the anvil," was greatly feared; see D. Hyde, *Religious Songs of Connaught* (London n. d.) 2. 284-86. Ample evidence to the same effect is found in the handwritten materials collected by the Irish Folklore Institute, Dublin.

[5] Lines 74-77 are in Latin.

INDEX

INDEX

abbot, 54, 99

abecedarian hymns, 58, 101

absolution, 87

adulterer, adultery, 51 f., 98

alienus, "excommunicated," 97

alms, of pagans not to be accepted, 51; of the excommunicated not to be accepted, 42, 51, 91

Ambrose, St., *De virg.* 1.3: 89

anathematization, 52

angel(s), 40, 46; messenger of God, 34; Patrick compared to, 61 f.

Annals of Ulster, 7, 17, 77, 100

Annals of Innisfallen, 17, 77, 100

Annals of the Four Masters, 78

Antiphonary of Bangor, 59

Apocalypse, 64

Apollinaris Sidonius, 83

apostata, 91

apostles, 46 f., 103; (St. Peter), 46; (St. Paul), 29; Patrick compared to, 61 f., 65, 103

apostleship of St. Patrick, 61 f., 103

Apostolic See, appeal to, 14

Aralanensis insola, 95 f.

árd-rí, 104

Armagh, 7, 14, 48, 104; date of foundation, 7, 14; compared to Rome, 101. See *Book of Armagh*

Armorica (Brittany), 76

Arrian, *Cyneg.* 1–3: 84

Attila, 75

Audite omnes. See Secundinus, St., *Hymn on St. Patrick*

Augustine, St., 90; contrasts Christ and *Sol Invictus*, 84; his *Confessions* known to Patrick, 9; other echoes of his works in those of Patrick, 15

    Enarr. in Ps. 75.2; 97.3: 103; *Ps. c. part. Donati*, 58; *Sermons*, 84, 88 f.

Auxerre, 5 f., 10, 76 f., 96

Auxilius, St., bishop, 6, 10, 13 f., 50, 57, 96

avarice, 43

Avrolles, 6

Bannauem Taburniae, 3, 21, 76

baptised faithful, 46; captives, 42, 45; women, 46 f.

baptism, 32–34, 37, 53, 63; solemn, during Easter Night, 98; rite, 41, 78; in Stowe Missal, 98 f.

barbarians, *i.e.* non-Romans, 101 f.

beatus, 89

benedictio (consecratio) virginum, 89

Benén. See Benignus, St.

Benignus (Benén), St., bishop of Armagh, 14, 69, 77, 104

Bethu Phátraic (Tripartite Life of St. Patrick), 18, 67, 101

Bible, treasured by St. Patrick, 64; text of St. Patrick, 11, 16, 90, 96; of St. Secundinus,

f., 25, 28, 38 f., 41, 61, 64, 101; religious training under St. Germanus at Auxerre, 5, 76 f.; deacon, 5, 29, 77; candidate for the Irish episcopate, 5, 30; sent as bishop to the Irish, 6, 41, 86, cf.29; "bishop by the grace of God," 41, 63; "teacher of the Irish," 61–64; missionary work, 6 f., 10, 31–39, 42–44; preaching, 102; before Laogaire, 104; had to change his language, 23, 81; spoke Gaelic, 81; teaches doctrine of grace, 10; converts Irish princes, 6, 34; escorted by sons of Irish kings, 37 f., 89 f.; spends money for admission to certain territories, 37; for guides, 37; persecuted, 32, 38; taken prisoner, 32, 37; dangers to his life, 31 f., 87; metropolitan see at Armagh, 7; metropolitan jurisdiction, 13, 48, 94 f.; appoints Fiacc bishop of Leinster (legend), 97; legendary conversation with Secundinus, 101; "approved in the Catholic faith," 7; cf. 35; "kept the faith," 35, 61; alleged journey to Rome, 7; opposed in Ireland and abroad, 7, 12, 29, 32, 44, 57, 79, 86, 102; refuses to accept gifts, 32, 37; defends himself against accusation of simony, 9, 36–38, 79; despised, 21, 41, 45; feels a stranger in Ireland, 21, 32; wronged by Coroticus, 7, 11; demands his ex-

communication, 12, 57 f.; criticised, 7, 9, 14, 29, 35 f., 57, 102; writes his *Confession* in self-defence, 9, 12, 79; defends his decision of writing it, 24; his lack of learning (*rusticitas*), 5, 8 f., 14 f., 21, 23 f., 31, 36, 40 f., 46, 81; fears the criticism of the learned, 23 f.; familiar with ecclesiastical legislation, 15; geographical knowledge, 87; held no chiliastic views, 87; head of the Irish Church, 101; "Christ's vicar," 64; given to the Irish by God (Christ), 25, 29 f., 35; treasures the Bible, 64; his Bible text, 11, 96; his liturgy, 10, 49, 78, 96, 98; sings hymns, psalms, 64; his "Creed," 22, 80 f.; said to have assisted in revision of *Senchas Mór*, 98; his death, 8; "model to the faithful," 62 f.; compared to angels, apostles, 61 f., 65; his intercession sought, 59; triduum of his *dormitio*, 59; devotion to him in 7th century, 100; "to judge the Irish at the Last Judgment," 103. —Describes himself as a sinner, 21, 29, 35, 40 f.; was indifferent to religion in early youth, 21, 29, 80; his early sin, 4, 6, 29; regards his captivity as punishment for his sins, 21, 23; his prayers, 4, 25, 31, 63, 65; spiritual prayer, 28 f.; mortifications, 4, 25; has visions, 28, 30;

ANCIENT CHRISTIAN WRITERS

The Works of the Fathers in Translation

Edited by

J. QUASTEN, S. T. D., and J. C. PLUMPE, Ph. D.